Green Living Made Easy

101 Eco Tips, Hacks and Recipes to Save Time and Money

NANCY BIRTWHISTLE

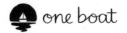
one boat

First published 2022 by One Boat
an imprint of Pan Macmillan
The Smithson, 6 Briset Street, London EC1M 5NR
EU representative: Macmillan Publishers Ireland Ltd, 1st Floor,
The Liffey Trust Centre, 117–126 Sheriff Street Upper,
Dublin 1, D01 YC43
Associated companies throughout the world
www.panmacmillan.com

ISBN 978-1-5290-8838-0

7 9 8 6

A CIP catalogue record for this book is available from the British Library.

Illustrations by Mel Four

Typeset in Adobe Caslon Pro by Palimpsest Book Production Ltd, Falkirk, Stirlingshire
Printed and bound by CPI Group (UK) Ltd, Croydon, CR0 4YY

This book contains the opinions and ideas of the author. It is intended to provide
helpful general information on the subjects that it addresses. Before following any
instructions outlined in this book, it is suggested that the reader undertakes a patch test to
ensure suitability and follows any relevant manufacturer or supplier guidelines. The publisher
and author disclaim all responsibility for damage, loss or injury of any kind resulting from
tips or instructions contained in this book. Handle materials with care. For use under
responsible adult supervision only. All necessary precautions should be taken.

Visit **www.panmacmillan.com** to read more about all our books
and to buy them. You will also find features, author interviews and
news of any author events, and you can sign up for e-newsletters
so that you're always first to hear about our new releases.

For all the children

Contents

Introduction

'If only I had the time . . .'

Have lives always been packed so full that there was never the time to get everything done? In years gone by, I realize tasks took much longer because there wasn't the luxury of labour-saving devices, cars, computers and the like. So why now, with all of our fancy gadgets, are we not twiddling our thumbs?

I have decided that to make time for the writing of this book my day needs to start that bit earlier, or does it? Should I instead realize that the day should be the same but that something else needs to take a back seat for a while? I'll let you know by the time I get to the last page . . .

More time, less waste and greener living, in a much broader sense, is what this book is about. Our planet is struggling and we need to use our resources, our money and our time wisely to try to change some of our ways for our own sakes, and for those of the generations that will follow. Our everyday life is under pressure as we continue to pack every minute with 'things' that seem to have to be done or bought. We need to think about waste, and that covers a whole range of topics – food waste, energy waste and the tons of decent, cast-aside reusable items that end up in landfill. Is it time to make do and mend again a little more often?

Our climate agenda is a dominant issue and many of us are wanting to make changes to support this. For some it may be a small change, whereas others are wanting to radically alter the way they work and live. The catastrophic Covid pandemic, which turned life as we knew it completely upside down, was also probably a catalyst for change for many.

Working from home and Zooming off to a meeting is now a thing for many people in a way that it never was before. We are learning that no longer can we take anything for granted. We are learning to value our time, value what Mother Nature has to give and understand that we cannot relentlessly take from our planet – we have to also 'give back' in order to try to reverse or at least halt some of the damage that we have caused.

I feel excited and inspired to share with you the following chapters. I have tried to put into words the ways I have changed and how I continue to examine my daily life. I will touch on a whole range of topics, including a number of upcycling craft ideas, easy recipes that will save money, time and energy, and a section on growing for those that may be completely new to the magic of nurturing and raising food from seed and cuttings.

Following on from my last book, *Clean & Green*, where I shared my journey, recipes and methods that have resulted in me switching to an eco-friendly clean home, I have added a number of new recipes, hints and tips that continue to prove to me that there is nothing I miss about harmful chemical cleaning products.

Finally, there are the important areas – our family, friends and ourselves. Let's have a little look at the good, simple, everyday food that we all know and love. With a few short-cuts, smart moves, easy to follow methods and recipes, plus a pinch of critical thinking, I can guide you through so that you can make it, love it and substantially reduce your food waste – saving money and time in the process.

While we're at it we can explore entertaining, but in a relaxed, confident way. You will see that everything in this book is affordable and fun – whether it's making your own table decorations, helping you to make a plan or offering tips for getting ahead – to give you the confidence and time to enjoy being with your guests. I have a number of home-made gift ideas, too, something that has become important to me, plus other tips and ideas that will not go on to cost the Earth!

Join me to take a look in the mirror and like what we see, knowing we are doing our level best for everything and everyone around us.

Let's go!

KITCHEN

My favourite quote:

I need to start in the kitchen!

In my home, the kitchen is the engine room of the house and also the warmest and most friendly place. Family and friends that pop by take a seat at my wooden table, have a cup of coffee or tea and a tasty treat from the biscuit or cake tin. Many a problem has been shared around this table – as well as jokes, laughter and, thankfully, not many tears.

At almost every waking hour, food is prepared in this room. It may be the daily meal cooking, but there is also baking, preserving, preparing or even just sitting with a pen and paper and scribbling down the planning of it all. This can be a list of seeds to order for the following spring, a meal plan for a celebration with friends or simply the week's supermarket shopping list.

This is the busiest room in the house, the one that takes up most of my time and, as a consequence, very often the room that produces the most waste. You may not spend as much time in the kitchen as me, but it's well known that this room is often the heart of the home. I decided that if I could tackle the waste produced in my kitchen, the rest of the house would be a doddle.

FOOD WASTE

We are told most days in the media about the amount of food waste generated each year and that we need to deal with the problem. I read that a staggering 6.6 million tonnes of food is thrown away in the UK every year. I find figures and statistics like this difficult to absorb, preferring to deal with my own food waste at a micro level and instead concentrate, simply, on my own fridge.

We all do it, go through the fridge and give it a sort out ready for the next supermarket shop. Shuffle the contents around, have a glance at the 'use-by' and 'best-before' dates, examine the dried-up piece of cheese, half-eaten bag of salad leaves and the black, gooey sludge at the base of the cellophane bag of rotted parsley. The food is popped into the compost (if there's the time) but more often than not the whole lot is tossed into the plastic-lined bin then out into another plastic-lined bin to end its life in landfill.

I didn't used to think about the life of the rubbish after it left my house or how, if I multiplied the waste I was producing by the millions of people doing the same thing, was impacting on our health and that of the planet. My refuse-disposing actions were robotic – daily rubbish into the (single-use) plastic-lined kitchen bin, then into the (single-use) plastic-lined dustbin and then off to be, thankfully, taken away by the refuse collectors.

I have never been more motivated to make changes in my daily behaviour than now, because I better understand how these automatic actions contribute to the problems. As the waste in landfill is rotting, it creates methane, a type of greenhouse gas that pollutes the atmosphere and goes on to contribute to global warming. In addition, all of my single-use plastic bin-liners will stick around in landfill for around 100 years.

I must just mention that very recently I have managed to completely dispense with plastic bin-liners even though I never thought I could. I know this will not be for everyone, it's just to let you know it is possible without being too onerous. I have two bins under the sink in the kitchen; one for compostable waste, veg peelings and the like, and the other for general waste, which corresponds with the refuse collection offered by my local council and my own garden compost heap.

For the general waste bin, I bought a reusable bin-liner made from cloth with a shiny interior, which can be washed when necessary. I use this for kitchen waste and I stack all of my empty flour and sugar paper packets, or in fact any paper bag, around the inside of this bin to protect the liner from food stains or spills. When I have any cooked food waste, or in fact any waste that is wet, sloppy or messy, it is transferred first into an empty flour or sugar bag, and a second bag if I think it could leak, before going into the fabric-lined bin. Once full, this bin is then emptied straight into my non-plastic-lined, large refuse bin, which is collected every two weeks. Everything in there is secure, is not going to leak or get smelly.

My second bin – for compost – gets everything else: tea leaves, coffee grounds, veg peelings, eggshells, orange peels, spent lemons, etc., and, other than a newspaper-lined base, that's it. This is emptied directly onto the compost heap outside. The bin, on emptying, looks unsightly, and this is mostly due to the scattering of a few remaining tea leaves that have stained and made the inside look yuck. After a quick swill under the cold tap,

I tip it out onto the compost then clean up using a cloth and a tablespoon of bicarbonate of soda. The bin is then left to dry outside for half an hour and it is as good as new.

The satisfaction for me is that I am probably reducing my contribution of plastic bags to landfill by around five or six per week (two from each kitchen bin and one large wheelie bin bag). Gosh – multiply that by millions of homes!

Note of caution, though! I tend to make rash decisions and stick to them. Deciding to dispense with bin-liners was one of those decisions that I made on a whim and had failed to communicate to him indoors. When I explained this to him afterwards (he had lined the empty bin outside with a liner) he first explained that he had no idea this was a house rule and then went on to produce a roll of fifty bags from the shelf and ask for suggestions! Maybe use up your stocks first.

When we consider trying to reduce food waste, the obvious solution would be to buy less, though that is easier said than done, especially with a growing family. Without a plan – and I have done this – there is the tendency to walk the supermarket aisles while randomly picking from the shelves those items, purposely positioned at eye level, which take your fancy. The 'two-for-one' offers, the '50 per cent extra' offers, the 'buy while stocks last' offers. Buying those 'just in case' items and, in particular, perishable packs.

I try so hard now to avoid food waste and this has to start when making the purchase – deciding what you *need* rather than what you *want*. My children know I used to preach to them the difference between a 'want' and a 'need!' Once the food has been purchased, it needs to be looked after and, most of all, used and eaten. I am hoping that after reading the tips in this chapter you will feel equipped to make the food you have bought stay fresh for longer, you'll be planning to buy only what you need and, ultimately, you will be saving money, drastically reducing your consumption of single-use packaging and bragging to your friends that throwing away food was something you used to do but never need to do now.

TWO-MINUTE SUPERSAVERS

Keep your shop-bought herbs fresh

To double the shelf life of your shop-bought fresh herbs, dampen a double-thickness sheet of kitchen paper with cold water. Lay on it either parsley, coriander, dill, thyme, rosemary or mint after removing from the packet. Roll loosely so that all of the sprigs are surrounded by a cold, damp blanket, then pop into an airtight box and keep in the fridge. I have had fresh parsley for almost two weeks kept this way.

Basil doesn't like the fridge and the leaves turn black. I find the easiest way to keep it fresh is to remove it from the pack, snip off the base of the stalks and place the sprigs in a glass of water on the windowsill. A plastic bag secured with an elastic band over the top, acting like a mini greenhouse, will keep them gorgeous for even longer.

Cheese

How often have you bought a large piece of cheese, and someone opens it, doesn't seal it thoroughly, then the next time it is visited and retrieved from the back of the fridge the exposed end is dry, hard and cracked?

A family will munch its way through a slab of cheese in one week, but for those living alone or in small households there is the temptation to buy smaller packs to save on waste. Smaller packs are always more expensive, so I continue to buy that large 400g (14oz) slab of cheese and when I open it and use for the first time I cut the rest of the block into approximately 100g (3½oz) pieces, pop one piece back into the original pack, wrapping it thoroughly, and into the fridge to use this week. The remaining handy pieces (and you will soon recognize exactly how big 100g (3½oz) is and won't need to get the scales out) I place into a strong plastic box in the freezer. Then for the next few weeks I have cheese that can be grated or used once thawed in the fridge for an hour or so.

Instantly you have reduced your plastic packaging, saved money, avoided food waste and have a ready cheese supply for sandwiches, pizza, snacks and salads. I can also cross cheese off my shopping list for the next few weeks.

A bought bag of grated cheese, once opened, needs to be used within about five days. After the first use, pop the whole bag into the freezer and use in the future from frozen. It remains free-flowing and will be good for another three months.

Milk

Going on holiday? An opened plastic bottle of milk still within its use-by date will freeze perfectly and needs only to be thawed overnight in the fridge when you get home.

Butter

I prefer butter on my bread, toast, scones and sandwiches rather than dairy spreads. I have read disturbing facts about the palm oil industry, so I try to steer clear of it when I can, although I realize it is in so many everyday products. It is hardly surprising that large populations of animals are being forced out of their natural habitat to make way for palm oil plantations.

My 250g (9oz) block of butter, kept in a butter dish during the winter months, is absolutely fine at room temperature of about 20°C and spreads perfectly, just as I like it. When the weather warms up, however, it is difficult to find a cool area where it doesn't get too warm and oily. The fridge is too cold and the butter sets like a rock and has to be sliced rather than spread to avoid it making holes in my fresh bread as I try to spread it. Dairy producers came up with a solution – flavourless oil is whipped into the butter (the taste is the same), a little more salt is added, then the mix is poured into a single-use container and once firmed up the butter blend can be spread straight from the fridge.

Spreadable butter is great but I cannot help thinking I am being slightly ripped off. When I examine prices and see that a paper-wrapped 250g (9oz) block of my favourite butter costs less than a plastic tub weighing the same, which is a blend of oil and butter, it had me thinking I would make my own. I get more for my money, I know exactly the ingredients that have gone into making it, I have been able to consume one less single-use tub and it tastes just the same.

This recipe yields a wonderful 350g (12oz) of spreadable butter and it lasts about a week in my house. You can make a half quantity if you are not huge butter-eaters. I have kept this for at least three weeks in the fridge. For those wanting to reduce their dairy consumption, this is the perfect compromise. This home-made blend still has the buttery taste even though the dairy is reduced by about a third.

You will need

roomy mixing bowl
hand-held electric whisk
butter dish
spatula

250g (9oz) your favourite butter (salted or unsalted)
a good pinch of salt (omit if you prefer unsalted butter)
100ml (3½fl oz) rapeseed or olive oil (use any flavourless oil)

Unwrap the butter, place it into the bowl and leave for an hour or so at room temperature until it becomes soft and the whisk will easily go through the butter to the bottom of the bowl when pushed. Turn on the power and cream the butter so that it is light and smooth, about 2 minutes. Sprinkle over the salt, if using.

With the motor running, add the oil in a thin, steady stream so that the fats emulsify and the mixture resembles pouring cream. Transfer to the butter dish, lift and bang the base of the dish onto the work surface to remove any air bubbles, then put on the lid and refrigerate for 1–2 hours. Once firm to the touch it is ready to use – spreadable butter straight from the fridge whatever the weather – and at around half the price!

This is the perfect affordable alternative to soft margarine and/or butter in your everyday cake baking. It creams readily, can be used straight from the fridge, is reluctant to curdle, contains no palm oil, no plastic packaging, is affordable – and gives the lightest sponge! Like cheese, butter, margarine and other fats will freeze perfectly.

Reusable Baking Parchment

When it comes to cake making I no longer take a deep sigh at the prospect of lining the base of the tin with greaseproof or baking parchment. A roll of reusable baking parchment has many uses and this one I favour above all others. Use the bases of your favourite cake tins as a template, then cut the reusable baking parchment to size. Washed between each use, this can be used over and over again. I use my two 15-cm (6-inch) sandwich tins most frequently and cake baking is even quicker as I reach for the tin and the base is already lined. Not only do I save myself a job, I am dispensing with a further single-use piece of paper.

Lumpy Sugar

How many times have you invested in a bag of dark brown sugar, used maybe 100g (3½oz) or so from it, then returned to the pack sometime later and found that it has set to a solid block?

There is no need to throw it away: simply unpeel the block of lumpy sugar into a heatproof bowl, cover with a dampened piece of kitchen paper, then pop into the microwave for a one-minute blast.

Remove the paper then take a wooden spoon or fork and break the softened sugar into lumps. Repeat, take from the microwave, leave for 30 seconds, then break any remaining lumps, using your hands if necessary to gently rub the sugar between the fingers until it feels soft and free-flowing again.

If you don't have a microwave, place the lumpy sugar in a heatproof bowl with dampened kitchen paper and cover the bowl with a plate, then put into a warm oven (set at around

50°C/120°F), which will soften hard sugar. How long it takes will depend on moisture levels. Check after half an hour and gently mix. Repeat until it is soft and free-flowing, breaking up any remaining lumps by rubbing between the fingers.

Once opened, always keep a bag of brown sugar in an airtight container to prevent clumping. I find a screw-topped glass jar perfect for brown sugars.

Flour

For those readers who seldom bake, cannot source self-raising flour, or have limited storage space, going out to buy self-raising flour when a recipe calls for it is really not necessary. You can create your own blend.

You will need

2 mixing bowls
fine-mesh sieve
large tin or airtight jar
500g (1lb 2oz) plain/all-purpose flour
15g (1 tbsp) baking powder

Stand a mixing bowl on your weighing scales and set a sieve over it, weigh out the flour then add the baking powder. Use a spoon to stir the flour and baking powder around within the sieve until the flour has transferred to the bowl underneath.

Then take the second mixing bowl and repeat: place the sieve over the bowl then add the flour and baking powder mix and use a spoon to stir within the sieve until the contents have transferred to the second bowl. It is important to sift the flour twice to ensure the baking powder is evenly distributed throughout the blend.

Transfer this 'own blend' into a jar or tin, mark as self-raising flour and use in any recipe that calls for it.

Trying to calculate the amount of baking powder to add to a particular recipe with plain flour can be disastrous, resulting in either a flat, unrisen cake or a cake with such a bad 'soda' aftertaste that for me it becomes inedible. Making up this 500g (1lb 2oz) flour blend is far more successful.

Bacon

I have to admit, although I adore vegetarian food and can embrace the vegan, I love a bacon sandwich. Fresh bread and crispy bacon – yum. Yet so often I discover an opened pack of bacon with maybe three rashers that are in great danger of either drying up or going off completely at the back of the fridge. I now keep a plastic box in the freezer, just a tiny one, but it comes in very handy. I cook off any of these random bacon rashers until they are crispy, then break them up into small pieces and pop them into this box in the freezer to keep. They make a welcome topping to pizza, and are delicious stirred into pasta and sprinkled over salads.

Herbs: Fresh or Dried?

Many recipes call for fresh parsley, coriander, tarragon or dill. If it's not a herb you think you'll use immediately beyond that specific recipe, you can opt for dried instead. I am always mindful that during the winter months many fresh herbs may have had to travel long distances before they reach the supermarket shelves.

Growing herbs at home during the summer then drying any surplus yourself and storing it in jars is a neat and thrifty way to keep supplies going. A dehydrator is brilliant for this, but if you don't have one, a microwave oven will do a sterling job in minutes. (See page 303 for details.)

For dried herbs, as a general rule, use half the quantity you'd need of fresh. If your recipe calls for 2 tablespoons of chopped fresh parsley, for example, 1 tablespoon of dried will be perfect. Similarly, bay leaves are nearly always sold dried. I have a bay tree in the garden so I never buy them as I can pick them fresh year round. If a recipe calls for a bay leaf, I go straight out to the tree, harvest two, fold them up and crease them to release their perfume, then they go straight into the stock pot.

A bay tree, however small, will not only look gorgeous in the smallest of gardens, or on a patio or balcony, the leaves will add distinct flavour to stocks, soups and sauces, and being evergreen, you will never run out.

Fresh Spice

How many times have you bought a bag of fresh chilli, lemongrass or ginger root, used the small amount required in your recipe, then returned to it a week or so later in the fridge to find it wrinkled, dried, discoloured and with maybe a touch of mould going on? Off it goes to be tossed onto the compost heap or into the bin.

I buy fresh ginger and lemongrass just once or twice a year and when I get it home I transfer it to a small plastic box and into the freezer. I break up the ginger root into chunks and grate both skin and flesh from frozen, then pop any unused root back into the box for next time. I grow chillies and freeze them once harvested and use from frozen. For lemongrass, I trim the root ends and leaves, then freeze and slice from frozen to use.

SUGAR

When I was growing up, the only sugar we had on the shelf was granulated and it seemed to satisfy our every requirement. I am pleased to say it still can. The supermarket shelves now stock all kinds of sugar, and some of it is very expensive.

For those who are not sure of their sugars, here is a reminder:

GRANULATED SUGAR consists of coarse crystals in the UK but in the US I gather granulated sugar is finer and commonly used in baking. In our house, granulated sugar is the everyday sugar-bowl sugar, mainly used for sweetening hot drinks and sprinkling over cereal. It tends to be the least expensive of all refined sugars.

ICING SUGAR is the finest powdery sugar that's perfect for royal icing, buttercreams and sweets. Non-gritty in nature, it flies through the air, covering work surfaces as it is so light.

CASTER SUGAR is fine white sugar and my go-to for most baking, particularly for cakes because it readily dissolves into the batter, resulting in a smooth and creamy mix. I also use it for certain buttercreams and meringues.

LIGHT BROWN SOFT SUGAR is as it says light, soft and brown with a caramel favour. It is perfect for the Green Tomato Cakes on page 166. I also use it when making chocolate buttercream

DARK BROWN SOFT SUGAR the colour says it all. Rich, dark and with a molasses flavour, it is used in gingerbread and Christmas cake.

It is not necessary to go out and buy all these sugars. We can make them! If you seldom bake, have limited funds, limited storage space or find yourself out of a particular sugar when you need it, this is a great tip for you. If you have a food processor, robust hand blender or liquidizer and a few storage jars, then we're rocking and rolling!

I had used this sugar-making method in an emergency when I had run out but, after looking at the price differences among specialist sugars, it makes absolute sense to do what I have come to call my 'kilo job' on a bag of granulated sugar as a matter of course. I bake a lot, though I rarely need more than 200g (7oz) of brown sugar at a time, so this is perfect.

This recipe lets us make a shelf of five sugars for a fraction of the price of individual bags. Home-made icing and caster sugars work out at around half the price of the bought versions, and home-made brown sugars can be up to a quarter of the price.

You will need

food processor, stick blender or liquidizer (for caster and icing sugar)
4 clean glass jars and lids (or any airtight containers)
jam funnel (optional)
glass marker pen or label
medium-sized mixing bowl
microwave oven

1kg (2¼lb) granulated sugar
8g (¼oz) cornflour
40g (1½oz) black treacle

Caster Sugar

Start by making the caster sugar. Weigh 200g (7oz) of the granulated sugar into the bowl of a food processor or liquidizer, or into a mixing bowl if using a stick blender. (I use a hand-held blender with its own blender attachment holding 200g/7oz exactly.) Blitz on the highest setting for just 30 seconds. The sugar is now finer in texture, perfect for baking and can be transferred to one of the jars using the jam funnel as an aid. Label it as Caster Sugar and move on to the next . . .

Icing Sugar

Weigh another 200g (7oz) of the granulated sugar into the processor or bowl and this time add 8g (¼oz) cornflour, which will keep the sugar grains separate. Blitz, this time for 2 minutes, and remove the cover from the blender and transfer the fine powdery result to a second jar. Label it as Icing Sugar.

Light Brown Soft Sugar

To make light brown soft sugar – weigh a further 200g (7oz) of the granulated sugar into a medium-sized mixing bowl and swirl over 15g (½oz) of the black treacle. (A warmed tin will ensure the treacle is easy to pour. In cold weather, stand it on or near a radiator for 15 minutes or so before using.) Stir the whole lot around with a spoon then pop the bowl of sugar into the microwave for 15 seconds. Use your hands to rub the sugar between your fingertips to completely incorporate the treacle. After about a minute the sugar will be transformed to a soft, light golden sugar. If you don't have a microwave, place in a warm oven at around 80°C (175°F) for about ten minutes to soften the sugar and treacle so you can easily rub it together with your fingertips. Transfer to the third container and mark Light Brown Soft Sugar.

Dark Brown Soft Sugar

For the fourth and final jar, take another 200g (7oz) of the granulated sugar and place it into the bowl already used for the light brown sugar recipe above, swirl over the remaining 25g (1oz) black treacle, stir around and then pop into the microwave again for 15 seconds (or in the oven as above). Rub in with your fingertips for a minute or so then transfer this deep, dark, gorgeous, caramel-scented mix into a jar marked Dark Brown Soft Sugar. On with the lid.

Granulated Sugar

Leave the remaining 200g (7oz) of sugar in the granulated sugar bag to be used as normal.

I'd say that is a very productive, money-saving use of half an hour. The added benefit is that I discard another item of single-use plastic packaging. Brown sugar is always wrapped in plastic due to the moisture content. Granulated sugar is usually packed in paper – this is definitely a win-win for the climate-conscious baker.

SALAD SUPERSAVER

You are hosting a barbecue. You got well ahead, had everything prepped and good to go. Drinks are chilled, there are plenty of ice cubes, salads are washed and dressed, cold desserts done, and the outside table looks gorgeous in the sunshine. The guests arrive, the barbecue goes on, lots of chat and fun, and then out comes the food. Everyone dives in and it all looks yummy, though your own eyes are drawn to the salad. The dressing that was added only about an hour ago has caused the leaves to go limp, some of the torn edges of the lettuce have turned brown and it doesn't look nearly as fresh and crisp as it did.

Here is the tip: spoon 2–3 tablespoons of your favourite dressing into the base of the salad bowl. Add your washed and dried salad leaves, putting the largest lettuce leaves first then adding smaller leaves such as rocket, coriander, basil, cress, mint or other mini herb leaves at the top. Cover with a plate and pop into the fridge.

When the salad is ready to take outside, remove the bowl from the fridge, and use salad servers or simply a spoon and fork to quickly toss the leaves, bringing the pool of dressing from the bottom of the bowl to the top and coating each gorgeous piece of green. Scatter over a clipping of fresh chives and the salad is fresh, crisp, glistening and gorgeous, and who would know you prepped it ages ago?

This is my 'go-to' lemon parsley salad dressing, sufficient for one large salad bowl.

You will need

screw-top jar and lid
around 2 tbsp very finely chopped fresh parsley leaves
3 tbsp rapeseed oil (or olive oil)
1 tbsp fresh lemon juice
1 tsp finely grated lemon zest
1 small clove of garlic, crushed
½ tsp salt
¼ tsp pepper
½ tsp Dijon mustard

Pop all the ingredients into the screwtop jar and shake. Taste, then add more oil if you prefer a smoother, less-acidic dressing. This dressing will keep for 4–5 days in the fridge.

MAGIC MAYO!

Mayonnaise is probably one of those accompaniments that most people buy rather than make. Home-made tastes amazing, though the downside is its short shelf life. Most recipes state it has to be refrigerated and eaten within five days.

However, can I convince you to make it yourself if I say we can make it in minutes, the recipe is simple, you can ring the changes with the flavours, there are no mysterious additives, yet the shelf life is one month?

The magic ingredient that makes this possible is the simple natural preservative whey protein. It is contained in dairy products and is also incorporated into other foods during the manufacturing process, but for us at home, and because we need only a tablespoon, it can simply be poured off plain yoghurt. We have all seen the watery liquid on the surface of a pot of plain yoghurt, which I usually stir back in, but to make this mayonnaise we need to harvest it.

I have a jar of this mayonnaise in the fridge all the time and spoon out a couple of tablespoons to turn it into garlic mayo when I want a kick with my jacket potato fillings or tartar sauce to have with fish dishes, and adding horseradish will liven up any sandwich.

I find it much quicker and easier to make mayonnaise with a food processor and mine has a handy small bowl that sits inside the main bowl for mixes such as this.

As with all fresh home-made mayonnaise, this recipe contains raw eggs. I have my eggs from my own chickens, but for those wanting to avoid eating raw egg, fresh pasteurized eggs are available, which will reduce the risk of food-borne illnesses in dishes that are not cooked or only lightly cooked. Pasteurized egg can be bought as a liquid product or as an egg pasteurized in the shell. Many mayonnaise recipes use only egg yolks but I have found one whole egg gives the perfect consistency, and no waste.

> **NOTE:** If your yoghurt is fresh and the whey is not separating easily, simply spoon off 2 tablespoons, place it onto a thin layer of muslin set over a tea strainer with a container underneath. Leave it for an hour and the whey will have dripped through. I return the strained yoghurt back into the big tub, give it a quick stir and there's no waste.

You will need

food processor
screwtop jar and lid
1 fresh egg or 50g (2oz) pasteurized whole liquid egg
1½ tsp dry English mustard powder or 1 tbsp Dijon mustard
¼ tsp garlic granules
¼ tsp salt
1 tbsp whey protein
200ml (7fl oz) rapeseed oil
½–1 tsp balsamic vinegar (or any vinegar)

Place the egg in the small bowl of the mixer with the blade attached then add the mustard, garlic, salt and whey protein.
Start the motor running and run for around 30 seconds until

28 · GREEN LIVING MADE EASY

well combined. Add ½ teaspoon of the measured oil and continue to mix, then add another ½ teaspoon and continue to add the rest of the oil in a very thin, steady stream. This will take a minute or so and as the oil is incorporated the mayonnaise will thicken.

Finally, add just ½ teaspoon of the balsamic vinegar, whizz again in the machine and then taste, adding more vinegar if you need it. If making one of the below flavour alternatives, add additional ingredients now.

Transfer to a clean jar with a screwtop lid and leave at room temperature for 8 hours. This gives the whey the chance to do its preserving work. After this time the mayonnaise can be transferred to the fridge and used as required. This mayonnaise will keep for up to a month in the fridge.

Flavour alternatives

For Aioli Sauce: an additional 1 tsp garlic granules or 1–2 cloves of crushed garlic

For Tartar Sauce: 1 finely chopped gherkin, 1 tbsp chopped capers and 1 tsp chopped parsley

For Horseradish Mayo: 1–2 tsp fresh grated horseradish (or to taste) and 1 tbsp finely chopped chives

NOTE: As with any jar of jam, mayonnaise, preserve or sauce (bought or home-made), always use a clean knife or spoon when taking from the jar to prevent contamination, which will lead to mould forming.

HEDGEROW PESTO

Here is a really handy recipe that will use up excess basil, rocket and parsley and any fridge salad leaves. It can also be supplemented with a little foraged wild garlic, dandelion and even nettles. I call it Hedgerow Pesto and it is beyond delicious. I make this pesto, then pop it into an ice cube tray and freeze. Once frozen, I pop out the cubes into a freezer box, then use one cube per person to stir through pasta or add to recipes.

You will need

rubber gloves (if using nettles)
tongs or blanching basket
food processor or blender
piping bag
ice cube tray
60g (2oz) leaves (any mix of basil, wild garlic, marjoram, oregano, dandelion, rocket, parsley, salad leaves, nettle tips, kale leaves – not stalks)
3 tbsp grated Parmesan cheese
1–2 cloves of garlic
25g (1oz) toasted pine nuts (or walnuts, hazelnuts or almonds)
½ tsp fresh lemon juice
100ml (3½fl oz) rapeseed or olive oil
salt and pepper, to taste

I blanch the greens when making a pesto. A quick dip in boiling water immediately wilts the leaves, making them easy to blitz, and it also retains their vivid green colour. The leaves are then more suitable for freezing because it stops enzyme actions that otherwise cause loss of flavour, colour, texture and vitamins. You can skip this step and simply blitz the leaves straight from the garden (apart from the nettles) for a quick fresh pesto, though this isn't as good if you intend to freeze it.

Start by bringing a pan of water to the boil then place all of the leaves into a blanching basket, if you have one, or just throw them in loose if you haven't. Have at the ready a sink full of cold water. Remember to wear rubber gloves if you are using nettles – well worth the effort, by the way, as nettles have more vitamins and nutrients than many other green veggies and the sting is destroyed during blanching. Blanch the leaves in the boiling water for just 30 seconds then either lift out the basket or use tongs to remove the leaves and immediately plunge the leaves into a sink of cold water to halt the cooking process.

Drain the leaves in a colander or the basket then dry on kitchen paper or a clean cotton tea towel, squeezing out as much water as you can.

Transfer the leaves to the bowl of the blender and add the Parmesan, garlic, nuts, lemon juice and salt and pepper. Blitz until you have a thick paste, then with the motor running pour in the oil in a thin, steady stream. Take off the lid and taste the gorgeousness!

This vivid green sauce can then be transferred to a piping bag to more easily fill an ice cube tray. Freeze, and once frozen, remove the cubes and transfer to a bag or box. Keep in the freezer for up to 6 months.

TIP: With bought pesto, the contents of the jar need to be used within five days of opening. So often this does not happen, and some weeks later you rediscover the jar with a furry layer of mould on the surface, resulting in the whole lot having to be wasted and thrown away. Instead, after using the first spoonful or two, transfer the remaining contents of the jar into an ice cube tray and freeze, in the same way as you would with home-made pesto.

BIN IT OR WIN IT!

When it comes to food waste there are times when, despite our best efforts, what promised to be a tasty treat, is suddenly ruined. Maybe something has gone wrong or you forgot to set the timer, and now food items have to be discarded.

Burnt toast is the first that comes to mind, and although my grandmother used to make an attempt at a rescue with a quick scrape with a knife outside to break off all of the black bits – on the whole burnt food ends up in the bin.

Several other 'mistakes', however, can be rescued, so before deciding to bin the spoils, read on.

Split Buttercream

You have done exactly as the recipe states but suddenly your buttercream goes from a smooth, silky bowl of loveliness to a mass of scrambled egg. A split buttercream and other such disasters can put the novice baker off cake-making for ever. Some recipe books suggest discarding that a split or curdled buttercream and beginning again. A bowl of expensive ingredients destined for the bin! No, wait – it can be fixed!

Take 1–2 tablespoons of the split mix, pop it into a small non-metallic bowl (a used and washed plastic yoghurt pot is perfect) then into the microwave oven for just 10 seconds until the mix has turned to liquid. With the whisk running in the split buttercream, pour in this melted mix in a thin steady stream. Your buttercream will be transformed back to a velvety smooth cream. Stress over.

Fresh Cream

Who recognises this typical scenario on Christmas Day? A willing helper offers to whisk the double cream for the trifle. However, too much talking, laughing or drinking, one whisk too many and your fresh cream is over-whipped and has turned to a clumpy mass resembling cottage cheese. Take 2–3 tablespoons more of fresh cream or cold milk and whisk slowly by hand, not by machine, and gradually the cream will return to its smooth lusciousness. The trifle is redeemed and so is the helper.

Ganache

Instead of a smooth, silky, shiny glaze, the bowl of chocolate has turned stiff and clumpy. Whisk in 2–3 tablespoons double cream to return it to its former glory.

Chocolate

Who says chocolate and water don't mix? If melting chocolate gets too hot, it will seize and become hard and dull. The chocolate clumps and fixes hard to the whisk or spoon. I find white chocolate has the tendency to seize more than dark or milk.

If this happens, boil the kettle, then add just 1 teaspoon of boiling water at a time and stir well between each addition until the chocolate is smooth and silky again.

The amount of boiling water required will depend on the mass of chocolate, though as a general rule I find 2–3 teaspoons boiling water added 1 teaspoon at a time is sufficient to rescue 200g (7oz) chocolate.

Over-salted!

How many times does a recipe advise to 'season to taste' or 'check and adjust seasoning', but how do you know your seasoning is the best it can be? It's easy to make a mistake. A pan of over-salted soup, an over-salted casserole or stew? No need to bin it or risk the family complaining and leaving it anyway. A spoonful of jam stirred through will soften the blow and no one will ever know.

TIP TO AVOID OVER SEASONING: After seasoning soups, stews and casseroles, ladle out a small amount into a bowl then add more salt and pepper and stir in. Taste and decide whether the extra seasoning has improved the taste or not. It is always possible to add a bit more if required, but harder to take away.

Stock Cubes

Don't discard a chicken carcass, you can use it to make stock. I tend to do this in my slow cooker, but you can also cook it on the hob by adding all the ingredients to a large casserole with a lid, or do it in a pressure cooker.

To the chicken carcass (whether it's cooked or uncooked from home-filleting) add an onion, cut in half (skin and all), a carrot (washed but unpeeled), stick of celery (or the leaves), a bay leaf and a few parsley stalks (if you have them) and pour in enough cold water to cover the contents.

If you are making stock in the slow cooker, pop it on the slowest setting and leave for 8 hours or overnight; if you are cooking this on the hob, bring to the boil and simmer for around 45 minutes. A pressure cooker will cook a stock in about 15 minutes.

A veggie stock gives an additional layer of flavour, too, and I find the easiest way to accumulate sufficient veggie bits for a stock is to keep a large plastic box or bag in the freezer and pop into it the ends of celery, parsley stalks, trimmings from onions and carrots, parsnips, pea pods, leeks, and in fact any tasty veg. Once I have accumulated a large box or bagful, I load the frozen offcuts into a large casserole pan, slow cooker or pressure cooker and simmer for half an hour on the hob, several hours in the slow cooker or 10 minutes in a pressure cooker.

If you are not ready to use it immediately, once strained, the stock will keep in the fridge for five days, though I often pop mine into the freezer, to be used later (up to a year) to provide a delicious wholesome base for future casseroles, soups, pie fillings and stews.

Making stock for small freezers

Freezer space is valuable and the trouble is multiple 500ml (17fl oz) pots of stock are going to occupy a lot of room. Concentrated stock cubes, however, do not. Once you have strained your home-made stock, return it to the pan and bring it to a fast boil. Continue to boil rapidly until the liquid is a quarter of its original volume.

I dip a clean plastic ruler into the liquid at the start. Say the depth of the stock in the pan is 10cm (4 inches), I let it boil until the depth is just 2.5cm (1 inch) – that is good enough for me.

Allow the stock to cool. It will be thicker and darker in colour. Pour into ice cube trays and freeze. Once frozen, pop out the frozen cubes from the trays into a freezer bag or box, which takes up much less space. Two home-made stock cubes weighing around 50g (2oz) each can then be added to stews and casseroles along with 150ml (5fl oz) water to make up to 200ml (7oz) fresh stock.

Eggs

Did you know you can freeze eggs? Many baking recipes call for the use of only egg yolk or only egg whites, leaving leftovers of both. I seem to always need frozen egg whites and wouldn't be without a supply of them. They freeze beautifully, thaw in a bowl at room temperature in an hour or so and will successfully whip up for your meringues, Swiss meringue buttercream and angel food cake. A handy tip is to freeze a single leftover white in a silicone tea cake mould, then transfer the mini-dome shape into a box. You can then reach for as many or as few as you need. I freeze egg whites for up to a year.

Egg yolks can be frozen, too, but they need a light sprinkle of salt or sugar to prevent them going rubbery. I rarely freeze yolks and instead mix a quick 'all in one' lemon curd, which will keep in the fridge for three to four weeks (see pages 134–5).

Reusable plastic liners

Save the plastic liners from empty packets of cereal. They can be used to separate almost anything and make a really good, free alternative to cling film. The fused seams of the bag are easy to unpeel and you have the perfect solution for pastry rolling.

Cereal-packet liners also make brilliant bread bags and freezer bags. They are great for wrapping sandwiches and for use in lunch boxes and picnics. Cereal-packet liners really are one of my favourite upcycling discoveries.

TIME TO COOK

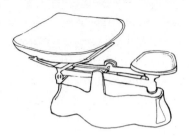

Part of every day of my life is spent deciding what to cook. I love food – growing, preparing, cooking and of course eating it.

Our task with the help of this book is to learn how to be smart cooks. I had, in my younger days, always to think about using energy wisely, but then there was only the one constraint for me, and that was cost. Money was tight and I had to watch the electricity and gas bill. As years went by and things got easier, the heating went on more often, the lights were left shining in every room and in fact, when it was dark out, the house seen from the outside used to resemble an ocean-going liner. When it came to cooking, the oven could be on with a casserole in it, two or three burners on the hob had potatoes and other veggies on them, and I'd use the microwave to quickly warm the plates.

I now find myself going back to basics and being mindful of my every action. Wasting valuable and finite energy has to be addressed if each of us is to help to save our planet. This book aims to help readers be smart by thinking about how we utilize our precious fuel, cut out unnecessary waste, grow some food, and include what we have grown in everyday recipes. And the results of all of these actions will also save us money.

I have a working week's easy oven-cooking recipes to share.

No hob, no microwave, just the oven. I used to think that the hob or stove top was the most efficient and least-costly way to cook but then I discovered that, in most cases, if more than one large burner is being used, it's actually cheaper and more efficient to use the oven. The oven uses less valuable energy, reduces cooking smells, has no pans boiling over and is less hazardous if children or pets are around. I have also found that oven-cooking frees up time – once everything is in there I can clear the work surfaces, wipe down, set the table, pour a drink and even sit and chat before the meal is ready.

Another handy habit to get into is turning the oven off ten to fifteen minutes before the end of the cooking time. Provided you don't open the oven door, the residual heat will be sufficient to complete the cooking, giving you at least ten minutes' energy for free.

My recipes are a collection of what I call 'Monday to Friday' meals that often find themselves on my menu. The difference between these and other similar recipes is that the whole meal is prepared, cooked and served from scratch, using only the oven and one pot. They are all on the table in about an hour.

The recipes are not meant to be complicated, outlandish or restaurant-style, rather they are my family favourites, which have been amended slightly to enable me to be hands and eyes off the cooking. I know exactly how long each dish will take and soon you will too. While the evening's meal is looking after itself, I can take a breather. Why didn't I cook like this before?

THE FOOD SHOP

When I was in full-time employment, a single parent with two teenage children, my weekly supermarket re-stock was carried out on Saturday morning as soon as the shop opened its doors at 7.30am. I found it tiring, stressful and expensive. Once I had taken everything off the supermarket shelves, loaded it into bags, put the bags into the car, there was then the unenviable job of putting it all away when I got home. Online shopping sounds much more civilized, though I do like to have a browse. Shopping this way, I always had a half-bag of wilting salad, a lone rasher of bacon and some slimy mushrooms by the end of the week, unused and destined for the bin.

Increasingly, people are choosing to order their meals from companies who pack exactly what you need in the quantities required for a particular recipe, then deliver it to the door. Sounds impressive, it's quick, saves on time, the food is fresh, it works out cheaper than restaurant or take-away, there is little to no food waste, *but* it is expensive and has to involve lots of single-use individual packaging items. If you are a fan, and I know many are, of this method of meal planning, the fact that you're sitting down and choosing your meals means you're already halfway there. Only one step further in the same direction is even cheaper and less wasteful (plastics and packaging). With a pen or screen in front of you, sitting and choosing from the file of colourful plates of food and ticking which ones you will order, you are listing what is taking your fancy.

Let us instead make our own list of meals for the week. If you decide to follow my menu plan, to get you started I have written out the shopping list so you're good to go! My shopping list serves four so you can scale up or down for your household. It covers five nights and includes buying full-size packs of every ingredient. Instead of giving only 1 teaspoon of mixed herbs for a recipe, I have included the cost of a whole jar. You may have your own family favourites that will slot in nicely instead and be part of your weekly plan.

Once you have embraced a green living style of meal planning, you will be astounded at your thriftiness, efficiency and organization skills. I am still a fan of pen and paper – I have a notebook in the kitchen drawer and jot items down as they run out, then make sure all these items are added to my weekly shopping list.

I have looked at prices of 'recipe box' dishes and compared them to my menu for the week's supermarket shop. After doing the comparison, I discover we can serve up Monday's One-pot Puttanesca (see page 51) for less than half the price of those of the meal-packaging companies. It's prep-to-plate in just one hour, which compares perfectly with the 'boxed-up' alternatives, and leaves us with no excess packaging.

I do wonder whether people who rely on 'recipe box' menus then have to go out and buy cupboard staples too? If so, they will be paying twice for certain ingredients.

PLAN YOUR WEEK

Take time to think about the week ahead. I usually give a little time to this on Sundays, but choose a day that works best for you. For parents, when children are small it may be jotting down their activities that week. Is there a party coming up and do you need to buy a birthday gift? What is going on at school? Are uniform, lunches and sports kit sorted? You will be ticking those boxes without even thinking about it.

For other full-time workers it is a scan over the diary for the week ahead, registering that one day could be a late one, one is a super-early start. Or perhaps there is a particularly difficult meeting ahead and you'll need to be on the ball, with lots of reading and prep to do.

Have a think then about the week's food. The worst scenario for me was coming home from work, particularly in the winter time, feeling cold, hungry and tired. I wanted food and some order at the end of what may have been a particularly stressful day. When children are small they cry a lot when they are hungry, the older children start raiding the fridge and cupboards looking for snacks, impatient and not caring one jot that you are tired, hungry and hankering after a bag of crisps yourself!

By having the evening meals for the week ahead planned on Sunday, knowing the ingredients are there because you did the shop on Friday or Saturday (see Shopping List for Five Nights on page 47) and the meal will be on the table within the hour, all takes off the pressure. I recall that on the days when I was in my Monday-to-Friday 9-to-5 I performed so much better when everything at home was in order. I could give my work the best simply knowing I had the evening's meal organized. That may sound ridiculous, but as a food lover, meal planning has always been relevant to me.

I am not suggesting you follow this plan every single week, but do it for starters and you'll see it works. You might have your favourite little menu plan and all that needs to be done is to organize it during your thinking time. And if things change in your week, swap the days around – if you work late one night, then Monday or Thursday in my plan will give you the quickest meals.

Having a box of ready-prepared crumble or a few puds in the freezer are a godsend if you need a little lift after a long day or, like me, you enjoy a sweet end to a meal.

Here's what my five-day menu plan looks like:

MONDAY: For those that work Mondays this is probably the most stressful day of the week. Let's have One-pot Puttanesca (see page 51) and a crumble. On with the oven and in with the meal's ingredients. While the meal is cooking, you could set the table, sort out the kids or maybe your outfit for the next day, and once you get familiar with the recipe there is even time for a shower!

TUESDAY: After having a look around the fridge, chopping up a few leftover veggies, an odd rasher of bacon or simply onion, cheese and dried or fresh herbs, we have a Crustless Quiche, Green Salad and Mini Roasties (see page 54). It is always handy to have yoghurt, and if you see it approach its use-by date a quick cake Lemon yoghurt cake (see page 141) can be thrown together in seconds.

WEDNESDAY: What to have on Wednesday? How about my Universal Chilli (see page 58)? All ingredients in the oven together – no pans bubbling over, no windows steaming up and on the table in no time. My quick apple tart (see page 177) could go alongside for pudding.

THURSDAY: Anyone for kedgeree (see page 63)? No precooking of fish, no cooking smells and topped off with an 'oven' hard-boiled egg, this is a tasty, classic plate of food. An oven-steamed pudding straight from the freezer, cooking alongside, will be a treat for hungry tums.

FRIDAY: Sausage One-pot (see page 66), or, for me, jacket spuds – see Time to Celebrate the Spud! on page 183 and choose from a selection of fillings.

I've provided some swaps to try to make these recipes suit different dietary requirements, but please use this as an invitation to play around and see what works for you. My shopping list and recipes serve four people but you can scale up or down, or freeze leftovers for another day.

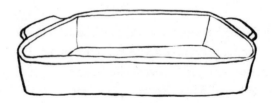

SHOPPING LIST FOR FIVE NIGHTS

SERVES 4

FRESH

250g (9oz) pack cherry tomatoes

2 lemons

90g bag salad leaves (see tip about keeping leaves fresh on page 25)

small pot or bag of fresh basil

3 fresh red chillies (or dried flakes or ones out of the freezer)

2–3 mushrooms

6 onions

4 carrots

2 parsnips

1 head celery

1 sweet potato

2.5kg (5½lb) potatoes (not too large)

2 apples

1 red pepper

2 garlic bulbs

500g (1lb 2oz) smoked fish (haddock, cod)

200g (7oz) king prawns (cooked or uncooked)

8 sausages (Lincolnshire, vegetarian, vegan)

50g bacon, chorizo or pepperoni

200g (7oz) lean beef mince (optional)

8 eggs

400ml (14fl oz) double cream

milk

400g (14oz) cheese (see note about freezing cheese, page 12–3)

100g (3 ½ oz) Parmesan

bag frozen peas (any size)

1 litre (34fl oz) apple juice

CUPBOARD AND DRIED

3 x 400g (14oz) tins tomatoes

1kg (2lb 4oz) fusilli or penne pasta

1 jar dried mixed herbs (18g)

1 jar dried rosemary (27g)

1 jar black sliced olives (saves time and often cheaper) (340g)

1 jar capers (190g)

1 litre (34fl oz) rapeseed, vegetable or olive oil

1 tub dried garlic granules (70g)

1 jar curry powder (38g)

1kg (2lb 4oz) packet of easy cook long grain rice

1 jar ground coriander (38g)

1 jar ground turmeric (45g)

1 jar cumin seeds (37g)

500g pack green lentils or Puy lentils

150ml (5fl oz) soy sauce (dark or light)

500g (1lb 2oz) cornflour

500g (1lb 2oz) brown sugar (or home made from granulated, see page 23)

2 x 400g (14oz) tin red kidney beans

1 x 400g (14oz) tin black beans

135g tube tomato purée

250ml (8fl oz) malt or apple cider vinegar

vegetable stock cubes or pots

LET'S COOK

To make optimum use of the oven, and before switching it on, I decide which pots will be used and therefore which shelves I will need. I get out all of the ingredients onto the work surface and have everything to hand.

My list of equipment for cooking a week's worth of meals is fairly succinct. The oven is our heat source so obviously the ovenproof cooking vessels take pride of place.

For oven cooking

ovenproof frying pan, saucepan or dish
   with lid
large ovenproof casserole dish with a
   well-fitting lid

23cm (9 inch) solid ovenproof flan dish
large deep roasting tin
baking sheet

Sundry kitchen items

digital weighing scales
roomy mixing bowls
vegetable knife
chopping board
wooden fork or spoon
slotted spoon
sieve
measuring jug
timer
grater
a plastic freezer box with lid

MONDAY – ONE-POT PUTTANESCA

Made from scratch and on the table in 45 minutes. Penne or fusilli pasta work really well for this 'one-pot' family favourite. There's no separate cooking of pasta and sauce – it all cooks together perfectly.

SERVES 4

You will need

A large, deep ovenproof dish, casserole or roasting tin with a lid – mine is an oblong Pyrex and measures 30 x 20 x 6cm (12 x 8 x 3 inches)

2 tbsp rapeseed or olive oil

4–6 cloves of garlic, unpeeled

pack cherry tomatoes (250g/9oz or similar)

a bunch of basil (60g/2oz), stalks finely chopped, leaves torn into shreds

1 fresh red chilli (or tsp dried chilli flakes) – or use a chilli from the freezer (see pages 19–20)

300g (10oz) dried fusilli or penne

1 tsp salt

2 tsp mixed dried herbs (or 4 tsp fresh home-grown if you have them – parsley/sage/rosemary/thyme)

400ml (14fl oz) boiling water

2 tbsp tomato purée

3 tbsp sliced black olives (pre-sliced are cheaper)

3 tbsp capers

2 x 400g tins chopped tomatoes

freshly grated Parmesan cheese, to finish

When you are ready to start, turn the oven on to 190°C/375°F/ gas 5 and boil the kettle. Add the oil to the ovenproof dish followed by the whole garlic cloves, cherry tomatoes, chopped basil stalks, plus the chilli or chilli flakes. Pop the casserole into the oven without a lid and leave it in for 20 minutes.

While the dish is in the oven, weigh the pasta into a bowl or heatproof jug, add the salt and dried (or fresh) herbs and pour over the boiling water – give it a stir then spoon on the tomato purée, black olives and capers over the top and set aside. Open and have ready the tins of tomatoes.

When the 20 minutes is up, take the hot dish from the oven and use a fork to gently squash the softened garlic – the pulp will pop out of the cloves, releasing the skin, which you can then remove. Squash the chilli in the same way, remove the core and mash the flesh. Now tip in the bowl of pasta plus the herby water containing the other ingredients. Add the tins of tomatoes and half of the torn basil leaves (reserving a handful to sprinkle over the finished dish).

Give everything a jolly good stir together, pop the lid on and then put back into the oven for 25 minutes to finish cooking. If you're making crumble for pudding (see pages 73-5) pop it in the oven now.

Remove from the oven, stir everything through before scattering over the rest of the basil and adding a grating of Parmesan cheese. Take straight to the table and serve on warmed plates. Turn off the oven, leaving the crumble, if making, inside to keep warm while you eat.

If you make this meal again next week, you'll only need to buy fresh tomatoes and basil – you have the rest in stock!

THREE-MINUTE SUPERSAVER

Your puttanesca is ready to serve, or maybe a take-away has arrived or your fish and chips, but you forgot to warm the plates and you don't want to risk your delicious meal going cold. Did you know that a spray of water on your plates and a three-minute blast in the microwave oven will warm them up in a jiffy?

If you are warming a pile of plates – six, for example – shuffle them around halfway through. Put the three top ones to the bottom, then the heat distribution is more even. If your plates have gold or silver decorations, or are made from pottery or terracotta, then do not use this method.

TUESDAY – CRUSTLESS QUICHE, GREEN SALAD AND MINI ROASTIES

A quick recipe, easier on the calories than versions involving pastry, and this is delicious hot or cold. Be flexible with the filling. Have a look around the fridge – bacon, cheese, mushrooms, peppers, tomatoes (I remove the seeds with a teaspoon to prevent a soggy filling), mild red chilli, chorizo, pepperoni, cream, milk – all manner of things can be thrown in, even a few leftover cooked green veggies, such as cooked fine green beans and peas. I have even used leftover cooked sprouts and sweetcorn. Cooking alongside will be a tray of 'mini roasties', and while these two are cooking you will have time to prepare a quick green salad to serve alongside.

SERVES 4

You will need

23cm (9-inch) solid ovenproof flan dish brushed with lining paste (see page 131)
ovenproof dish or frying pan

FOR THE QUICHE
50g (1 ¾ oz) bacon, or chorizo or pepperoni
2-3 mushrooms, finely chopped
1 onion, finely chopped
any mix of other ingredients to fill the flan dish to just over halfway (see intro)

1 tbsp vegetable oil

4 eggs

400ml (14fl oz) liquid (use 250ml double cream and make up
the rest using milk or single cream)

200g (7oz) grated cheese (any cheese, grated)

1 tbsp mixed dried herbs and/or chopped fresh chives/slices of
fresh or frozen mild chilli to top off (see page 12 for tips for
keeping them fresh)

salt and pepper, to taste

FOR THE MINI ROASTIES

2 tbsp vegetable oil

1kg (2¼lb) potatoes

1 tsp garlic granules

1 tsp dried mixed herbs

green salad, to serve

Pop the oven on to 200°C/400°F/gas 6, with the shelves on the
second and bottom runners down. On the upper shelf place the
small ovenproof dish or frying pan containing the oil, bacon (or
chorizo or pepperoni), cut into tiny pieces with scissors, plus
the chopped mushrooms and onion. Those items will start to
fry as the oven heats up. Allow to cook for 20 minutes. In the
meantime, prepare the rest of the ingredients for the quiche
plus the mini roasties.

Now make the quiche. Break the eggs into a measuring
jug, give them a beating then add seasoning and the measured
amount of cream and/or milk. Have ready any other bits you
have sourced to add to the quiche, such as red/green/yellow
peppers cut into 2.5-cm (1-inch) pieces, a few peas or any

leftovers as listed above. Sprinkle half of the cheese over the base of the flan dish and a sprinkle of chives and dried herbs, then season with salt and pepper.

Next, prepare the roasties. Place the oil in the base of a roomy mixing bowl, wash and dry the potatoes and cut into 5-cm (2-inch) dice. Toss in the oil in the bowl (I use my hands to coat each potato piece), sprinkle with salt and pepper, a teaspoon of garlic granules and a teaspoon of mixed dried herbs. Once all is well coated, transfer to a baking sheet and put into the oven on the lower shelf and set the timer for 35–40 minutes.

Take the dish or frying pan out of the oven and transfer the browning and softened onion, bacon and mushrooms into the flan dish to cover the cheese. Spread around in an even layer then add your choice of other ingredients to bring the filling depth to just above halfway in the dish. Pour over the egg and cream mix, the rest of the cheese and top off with a sprinkle of fresh or dried herbs. Add a few slices of mild red chilli (fresh or frozen) at the end to give a colourful zing to the finished quiche.

Put straight into the oven and bake for 30 minutes. Your roasties and quiche will be cooking together, giving you time to prepare a quick green salad.

I actually call lots of concoctions 'green salad', and in my house the salad may be cold or warm depending on the season. During the summer months I use a simple bag of mixed leaves as a base, and if I have them I will add a few chopped spring onions, cubed cucumber, sliced green pepper, thinly sliced celery or even just a scattering of fresh herbs (see tips in Time to Grow chapter). In the winter months when salad leaves may be imported, expensive and pretty tasteless, then it will be lightly steamed, finely sliced green cabbage or kale with a few chopped toasted nuts and sesame seeds sprinkled over. Stir through then add a few tablespoons of salad dressing (to either the cold or warm salad). I have included an easy home-made salad dressing recipe on page 26 that will also gloss up these cold or warm 'green' salads.

When the quiche is risen, browned, bubbling and smelling amazing, remove from the oven, transfer to a cooling tray and allow to rest for 5–10 minutes before cutting. During this time the quiche will firm up and be easier to portion.

Remember to turn the oven off 10 minutes before the end of the cooking time. While your quiche is resting, leave the potatoes in the oven with the door left slightly ajar.

If you decide to make this recipe next week, you won't need to buy more cheese.

WEDNESDAY – UNIVERSAL CHILLI
WITH JACKET POTATOES OR OVEN RICE

A recipe that manages to tick so many boxes – and I love it. I have named this my Universal Chilli because it can be adapted to fit just about every palate. Make with meat or flip a few ingredients and the plate becomes vegan, vegetarian, gluten-free and dairy-free. This recipe will feed six to eight people and, because it freezes well, I batch-cook this pot of food so there is always something to fall back on when you arrive home late.

This dish will cook alongside jacket potatoes or rice in the oven, freeing you up to do other things while the meal is ready to take to the table.

This chilli is perfect for freezing so I have upped the recipe to serve more than 4.

SERVES 6–8

The secret to depth of flavour is good-quality stock, so buy the best-quality stock pots or cubes or, even better and cheaper, make your own. (See tip on pages 35–6.)

You will need

A large, deep ovenproof dish, casserole or roasting dish with lid
Ovenproof saucepan or dish with lid
3 tbsp oil (I use rapeseed but any cooking oil will do)
2 onions, finely chopped
2 cloves of garlic, chopped

1 celery stick, very finely diced

1 carrot, finely diced or grated

1 tsp cumin seed

1 tsp ground coriander

2 tsp dried mixed herbs

100g (3½oz) Puy or dried green lentils, or 200g (7oz) lean
minced beef

500ml (about 17fl oz) good hot vegetable stock (home-made or
using quality stock cube) – 400ml (14fl oz) for meat version

1 red pepper, deseeded and cut into dice

1 fresh (or home frozen) chilli chopped, ½ tsp dried chilli flakes

2 x 400g tin red kidney beans and 1 x 400g tin black beans (or 3
tins red kidney beans)

1 x 400g tin chopped tomatoes

2 tbsp tomato purée

salt and pepper, to taste

fresh coriander to serve, if you have it (optional)

FOR THE OVEN RICE

300g (10oz) easy cook long grain rice

1 tsp salt

500ml (17fl oz) boiling water

NOTE: If making the chilli using lentils they need to be
rinsed well in cold water first. I place them into a sieve
and wash under cold running water then leave them to
drain over a jug. If you decide to serve the chilli with rice,
this too has to be rinsed well in cold water to ensure
separate grains. You can do this well in advance.

For this oven meal I cook everything together, so I organize the oven shelves before I start. The casserole dish for the chilli will go on the base of the oven along with the jacket potatoes or lidded pot for rice, but then I will use a shelf on the second runner from the top to bake a crumble or other chosen pud, if making. Once you have switched to oven- over hob-cooking and done it a few times you will know exactly how to space your pots.

Once the oven is organized, preheat it to 200°C/400°F/gas 6 and add the oil to the casserole dish and set it onto the base of the oven, without the lid.

While the oven is heating, prep the vegetables. The smaller the vegetables are chopped, the more flavour will be released, so try not to rush. Chop the onions first and set aside. Carrot takes time to cook through, so either chop it into very small dice, or grating is ideal. (Carrot, onion and celery combined add a delicious layer of flavour to any casserole. In French cooking the combination of onions, carrot and celery are referred to as a *mirepoix*. Mirepoix is also a small town in the south of France – just saying!)

The oven should now be to temperature after about 15 minutes, so quickly remove the casserole dish, add the onions, give them a quick stir in the oil and pop the casserole back into the oven for 5 minutes.

When the 5 minutes is up, take the casserole dish from the oven, remembering to close the oven door and keep the valuable heat in, then add the garlic, carrot, celery, spice and herbs. Stir them around then pop back into the oven for another 5 minutes. If making the chilli using minced beef I add it in at this stage too, breaking it up well among the onions and veggies and giving a good stir. While the veggies are frying in the oven, prepare to add the rest of the ingredients.

If using stock cube or a stock pot make up the stock by adding boiling water from the kettle. Take the casserole from the oven and this time add the lentils (if not using meat) and the hot stock. If making the meat version of this dish add only 400ml (14fl oz) of stock. Give a good stir, then pop the lid on, put it back into the oven and leave for 25 minutes. During this time the lentils will absorb the stock and become plump and tender.

During this time, prep the rest of the ingredients: chop the pepper and the chilli if using fresh or frozen, drain the beans (I rinse mine through a sieve), and have everything to hand.

If you are serving with rice rather than potatoes, prepare the rice now. Place the drained rinsed rice into an ovenproof pan or dish, add the salt then pour over the measured boiling water. I find it easier to place the pan onto my measuring scales and pour the boiling water directly over the rice. Immediately pop the lid on and slide onto the base of the oven alongside the chilli. The rice will need 30 minutes cooking time.

As the rice goes in, take the chilli pan from the oven, give it a stir then add the chilli (reserve a little to garnish), tomatoes, tomato purée, beans and red pepper. Pop the lid on and the dish back into the oven to cook alongside the rice for 30 minutes.

Taste and check the seasoning – adding more salt, pepper or chilli if necessary. If the rice is ready ahead of time, it can stand with the lid on on the work surface and will stay hot for 15 minutes or so.

I then like to thicken the chilli (without using flour or another thickening agent) by spooning out a cup or two into a separate jug and blitzing to a purée with a stick blender. Pour this back into the chilli and stir to thicken.

Serve with rice and a garnish of fresh chilli and coriander leaves if you have them.

If you don't fancy rice, this chilli is also great served with jacket potatoes, cooked alongside in the oven. If you plan to serve your chilli with jacket potatoes, have them both ready at the same time. Wash and dry the potatoes, prick with a fork and pop them into the oven when you switch it on. I have detailed my method for the perfect jacket on page 202 – crispy on the outside and meltingly soft on the inside – but here's a shortcut.

When time is tight and hunger bites, the baking of jacket potatoes can be sped up with a microwave oven, although this does add another appliance to our 'oven-cooking' method. Prick four washed and dried potatoes, weighing around 160–180g (5–6oz) each, with a fork then microwave on High for ten minutes while the conventional oven is getting to temperature. Take from the microwave using a gloved hand (they will be super-hot!), spray the skins quickly with oil then transfer to the oven to sit alongside any dish to finish baking, brown and crisp up. This will reduce the oven cooking time from 1 hour to around 30 minutes. If you're cooking a very hefty jacket potato, this is a great way to reduce cooking time and cut down on fuel.

This is a huge pot of chilli! Leftovers will keep for five days in the fridge or up to a month in the freezer. Next time you make a batch, you already have the herbs, spices, purée, lentils and rice, if using, in stock and can tick them off your list.

THURSDAY – KEDGEREE WITH OVEN EGGS

This is a classic dish, but one I used to find dry and a bit repetitive. My recipe includes interesting flavour tones to make this a great quick supper dish for four.

I used to use three burners on the stove for this: one to cook the fish, one to cook the rice and one to hard-boil eggs. Now, as we start to think and cook smarter, this menu can be served up as before, but to save on fuel and time, everything can be cooked together in the oven in a lidded casserole dish, with no pans boiling over. There is even time to have a shower, set the table and pour the wine while it cooks.

SERVES 4

You will need

A large, deep ovenproof dish, casserole or roasting dish with lid
Ovenproof saucepan or dish with lid
300g (10oz) easy cook long grain rice
4 tbsp oil
1 small onion, chopped
500g (1lb 2oz) skinless smoked fish fillets (check what can be sourced sustainably in your area. Haddock, cod or any similar alternative will work well. Smoked fish is traditional and the most flavoursome.)
200g (7oz) king prawns
600ml (20fl oz) boiling water
grated zest of 2 lemons, plus the juice
2 tbsp mixed dried herbs

1 red chilli, finely chopped

2 tsp curry powder

2 tsp ground turmeric

2 tsp cumin seeds

2 cloves of garlic, chopped small

4 eggs (1 per person – the older the better for hard-boiling)

2 teacups of frozen peas, set aside to thaw

4 tbsp double cream

a handful of fresh herbs to serve, if you have them (optional)

Place the rice in a sieve and rinse well under cold water, then leave to drain until dry and free-flowing again. If you don't have the time, simply rinse the rice under cold water and set aside until it is needed. Rinsing removes excess starch and I have found that if the rice is then left to dry, it is free-flowing when it goes into the pan and then non-clumped and free-flowing when cooked.

Put the oven on to 180°C/350°F/gas 4, add the oil to the casserole dish, add the onion to the pan, stir around, then transfer to the oven without a lid for 10–15 minutes until the oven has heated and the onion is sizzling in the pan.

During this time, cut the fish into 2-cm (¾-inch) dice, boil the kettle and have to hand all of the other ingredients.

After the 15 minutes, take the casserole dish from the oven, give the onion a stir then add all of the ingredients apart from the thawing peas, cream and fresh herbs. I start with the fish and prawns then the rice followed by the lemon zest and juice, the herbs, spices and garlic. Give a good stir then pour over the measured amount of boiling water. On with the lid then into the oven for 25 minutes.

Meanwhile, take the eggs, pop them into an ovenproof lidded pan or bowl and pour boiling water down the side of the bowl rather than directly onto an egg to prevent it cracking. Pour on sufficient water to cover the eggs then pop on a lid or plate to cover and put alongside the casserole dish in the oven. After 25 minutes, take the casserole dish from the oven, remove the lid, give it a stir and check to make sure the rice is fully cooked. It may need another 5 minutes.

When the rice is fully cooked and most of the liquid absorbed, stir through the peas and cream, then sprinkle over the fresh herbs. Taste and check the seasoning.

Turn the oven off, pop the casserole dish back into the oven to keep warm along with serving plates. Take the bowl of eggs from the oven, remove from the water with a slotted spoon, plunge into a bowl of cold water, then peel off the shells.

Serve the kedgeree with the boiled eggs, halved, over the top – delicious.

FRIDAY – SAUSAGE ONE-POT

This is a one-pot wonder in my opinion. Satisfying and warming, it tastes yummy and everything is in the oven together in a single large roasting dish. This dish can easily be scaled up as necessary. Here are the ingredients sufficient for a family of four. Use vegetarian, gluten-free or vegan sausages if you prefer – the rest of the recipe just falls into line. My dish measures about 30 cm x 45 cm and is 7 cm deep.

SERVES 4

You will need

A large, deep ovenproof dish, casserole or roasting dish
1 tbsp oil
4 cloves of garlic
8 sausages (2 per person) – pork, vegetarian, vegan, gluten-free
2 onions
2 celery sticks
2 carrots
2 parsnips
1 small sweet potato
12 small potatoes (small, egg-sized), or 3 large
2 apples
2 tbsp brown sugar
2 tbsp soy sauce
1 tbsp mixed dried herbs or 2 tbsp finely chopped fresh parsley/ sage/thyme
1 tsp dried rosemary or a fresh sprig, chopped

2 heaped tsp cornflour

500ml (17fl oz) apple juice

1 tbsp vinegar (apple cider or malt vinegar)

a handful of frozen peas

a good sprinkle of chopped fresh (or frozen) parsley,
    to garnish if you have them (optional)

Pop the oven on to 200°C/400°F/gas 6. Take a large roasting dish, add the oil, garlic cloves (unpeeled) and sausages then transfer to the oven as it comes to temperature for 15–20 minutes until the sausages start to colour and golden on all sides.

Meanwhile, prepare the vegetables. As each veg is prepped, pop into a large mixing bowl. Quarter the onions then remove the outer layer of skin. Cut the celery into 2.5cm (1-inch) lengths. Peel the carrots and cut into 5mm (¼-inch) slices. Peel the parsnips and sweet potato and cut into 2-cm (¾-inch) dice. Cut the potatoes in half, there's no need to peel. Peel and quarter the apples, core then cut each quarter in half, widthways. When all the veg is in the mixing bowl, add the sugar, soy sauce and herbs. Give everything a good mix – I find it easier to use my hands.

Take the roasting dish from the oven and pile the mix of sweet coated veggies into the same tin. Pop the dish back into the oven for 30 minutes or until the veg are tinged brown at the edges and just tender when spiked with a knife.

While that's roasting, spoon the cornflour into the base of a measuring jug then add the apple juice, a little at a time so that lumps don't form. Give it a good stir then add the vinegar.

Take the tin from the oven then sprinkle over the frozen peas and pour over the cornflour, apple juice and vinegar mix and pop back into the oven for just 10–15 minutes while the peas heat through and the sauce bubbles up and thickens.

Remove from the oven, sprinkle over the parsley, if using, then it's straight to the table to serve on warmed plates.

COOK-ALONG PUDDINGS

You might not always fancy a pudding but more often than not, I do! Each of the following recipes will cook beautifully alongside the weekday recipes without using up precious extra energy or time.

OVEN-STEAMED SPONGE PUDS

Who doesn't love a steamed pudding? Easy, economical comfort food for all the family and while the oven is on with the One-pot Puttanesca or any other one of my oven recipes, our puddings can go alongside, or they can go straight into the oven following the main course, to be steaming for 25 minutes while the family are eating. These puddings freeze extremely well, so you can eat some, freeze some or, one rainy Saturday, make them all for the freezer – a great quick pud to come home to midweek.

Normally with steamed puddings, a sturdy lid of baking paper and foil tied with string is required to avoid the puddings becoming soggy. However, because these are cooked in the oven, there isn't an excess of moisture and so they don't need an extra lid – saving on those single-use items.

You will need

6 x 200ml (7fl oz) mini pudding tins or ramekin dishes brushed
   with lining paste (see page 131) or a 550ml (1 pint/19fl oz)
   pudding basin
hand-held electric whisk
a casserole or ovenproof dish with a well-fitting lid large enough
   to accommodate the tins, ramekins or pudding basin with the
   lid on
6 tbsp golden syrup
125g (4½oz) soft butter or margarine (see home-made
   spreadable butter on page 14)
125g (4½oz) caster sugar (make your own – see page 21)
2 eggs
1 tsp vanilla extract
125g (4½oz) self-raising flour (see home-blended on page 17)

Place a tablespoon of syrup in the base of each pudding tin or
ramekin dish or add all of the syrup to the bottom of the large
pudding basin.

In a mixing bowl, whisk together all the remaining ingredients using the mixer until smooth and well combined. Use a
spoon or ice-cream scoop to divide the batter equally between
the six tins/ramekins or to spoon into the pudding basin.

If you just need two for now, freeze the other four in the tins,
then oven-steam from frozen for 30 minutes.

Place the pudding/s into the pan or casserole dish, then pour
boiling water down the side into the pan (careful not to splash
the puddings) so that it reaches about 2.5cm (1 inch) up the

side of the tins or basin, then quickly on with the lid and into the oven. These puddings will be steamed in 25 minutes (or an hour for the single pudding) – no steamer, no runny windows, no pan boiling dry, no extra fuel being used.

VARIATIONS

Jam Sponge

Replace the 6 tablespoons of golden syrup with your favourite fruit jam.

Lemon Sponge

Add 6 tablespoons of lemon curd to the mix and replace the vanilla extract with 1 teaspoon of Sicilian lemon extract.

Raspberry Ripple Sponges

Once the batter has been mixed, add 150g (5oz) crushed frozen raspberries to the final stir for a raspberry ripple sponge.

Chocolate Berry Sponges

This recipe is my favourite. Replace the self-raising flour and golden syrup with the following ingredients:

110g (4oz) self-raising flour (see home-blended on page 17)
25g (1oz) cocoa powder
⅛ tsp Chinese five spice
½ tsp instant coffee powder
1 tsp vanilla extract

50ml (2fl oz) milk

150g (5oz) frozen raspberries or blackberries, crushed to a crumb

(It is important to crush the frozen berries to ensure even baking and no soggy batter.)

Don't be frightened to play around with flavours, use stewed fruit in place of the syrup or add ground ginger to the dry mix for an autumnal version.

FROZEN OR FRESH FRUIT CRUMBLE

If you want to bake a quick pud while the oven is on, this is quick and easy – especially if you use a batch of already made and frozen crumble mix. I have a plastic box in which I keep crumble mix in the freezer, so this is the quickest 'go-to' pudding. Use fresh or frozen fruits and a layer about 4–5cm (1½–2 inches) deep in an ovenproof dish of any size is all you need. The fruit will reduce as it bakes and softens.

Take a look in the fruit bowl and rather than resigning those wrinkled apples, pears or peaches to the kitchen compost, enjoy them in a crumble instead. In addition, use any fruit that is in season or, alternatively, always have a bag of frozen berries to either fill in the gaps or use exclusively. I will not be prescriptive about weights – look instead at the dish you will bake it in. The dish needs to be about 7.5cm (3 inches) deep.

Slice the fruit and lay over the base, remember apples soon turn brown, so have everything ready before slicing them up and popping them into the dish. I sprinkle 1–2 tablespoons of sugar over apples and pears and maybe add a further tablespoon to fruits that are tart, like rhubarb and gooseberries.

Take the box of frozen crumble and with a large spoon scoop some out and gently lay it over until all the fruit is covered. Don't press it down, we want a crumbly crumble. Put the dish onto the top shelf of the oven at about 180°C/350°F/gas 4 – it will need 25–30 minutes to cook the fruits and bake the topping to a golden brown. Crumble isn't very fussy about oven temperature so it can likely go in with whatever else you're cooking, but it is best on the top shelf to ensure a satisfying crumble crust.

BATCH CRUMBLE TOPPING MIX

You will need

a very large roomy mixing bowl

a plastic freezer box with lid

500g (1lb 2oz) self-raising flour (or use your own blend – see page 17)

4 tsp either ground ginger/cinnamon/nutmeg or a mix of all three! (optional, though each makes a great addition)

200g (7oz) butter at room temperature (or spreadable butter – see page 14 or coconut oil for a vegan version)

200g (7oz) sugar – (use Demerara, granulated or home-blend soft brown sugar – see page 21)

200g (7oz) porridge oats, rolled oats or oatbran

Weigh the flour into the bowl then add the spice (if using) and stir through using a blunt knife. Add the butter, then use your fingertips to rub the fat into the flour as though making pastry. The mixture needs to look like coarse breadcrumbs with irregular lumps. Stir through the sugar and porridge oats.

The crumble is now ready to use or it can be transferred to the freezer box. Use from frozen – no need to thaw first.

There you have it – dinner for the week sorted. You may already have your own family go-to recipes and once you start to think differently about how to cook them you will discover, I am sure, that most meals can be cooked in the oven side by side with less effort, time and cost.

Those foods that we considered to be hob- or stove-top-only cooking are now looking after themselves in the oven. Rice, pasta, steamed puddings, boiled eggs, root veggies all cook perfectly, safely and more economically. You can even do mash in the oven – see page 195.

An added bonus is that the oven, unlike the hob, will give us at least 10 minutes of free cooking time, so try to get into the habit of turning the oven off 10 minutes before the end of time. Your oven will retain the heat and you will complete the final cooking stages of your meal for free.

I now set my timer routinely for 10 minutes less than the allotted cooking or baking time. When the timer rings it is my alert to turn off the power – setting then a further 10 minutes to remind me to remove my finished dish. I do this for bread, pastry, cakes, casseroles, roasts, Yorkshire puddings – in fact, I do it for everything!

TIME TO UPCYCLE, REUSE, REPAIR AND RECYCLE

We have all been guilty of the quick fix, and by this I mean throwing something out and buying a new one! Is there any wonder that we do this when the cost of a replacement item can be as cheap as a repair? I have even been told that economical repairs of certain items are not possible – for my printer, for example. Surely this has to change?

Going back fifty years, there was a typewriter repair man that used to come and service our old manual typewriters that had been in the office for decades. Can we not make items that last anymore?

We know now that the hidden cost is the planet's health and well-being, as more and more plastic packaging, component parts and other non-recyclable items are being dumped into landfill and will hang around for centuries. The demand for new, cheap replacements and the processing of all of these products continues to pollute our atmosphere.

If we stop and think, there are so many items that can be repaired, reused, recycled, upcycled – some of these are fairly new words in our vocabulary and are quickly becoming adopted and enjoyed, by me especially.

The focus is now very much on reducing waste and some

fantastic innovative ideas and products will, I am sure, in time replace the way we consume at the moment. For me in my small life, I examine each item before it goes into the bin and consider whether it has a further use – here are a few ideas.

HANGING PLANTER

My latest upcycling project has been the creation of a plant hanger using a plain white plastic 1-litre bottle that had contained vegetable glycerine. The bottle had lasted two years and rather than throw it into the recycling bin I reached for the string and a few coloured pens.

This is a great project for getting the kids involved in growing – painting a face and planting the planter is great fun, and naming the finished character adds a certain charm.

This planter has been in use well over six months and I will not discard it – I absolutely love it. It makes me smile every time I see it, and now a previously pot-bound supermarket thyme plant has room to spread its roots. See a little sketch of her opposite. I called her Medusa, but instead of long hair turned into venomous snakes we have a fun finish to a very uninteresting pot of thyme and a second home for a discarded plastic bottle. The planter can also be used for seed sowing, of course, which is another fun project with kids – watch the hair grow!

You will need

1 x 1 litre (34fl oz) white plastic squeezy bottle
craft knife or sharp blade
metal skewer or other sharp-pointed object
1m (3 ft) string and metal ring (if you have one), for hanging
multi-surface permanent marker pens (I used the pens I bought
   for glass painting my cleaning bottles)

few pebbles or a handful of gravel for drainage

peat-free compost

any plant in a pot no wider than the width of the bottle – spider
plant, cactus plant, thyme, mint – lots of 'hair-like' growth is
great fun

Start by washing the bottle thoroughly, then once dried use a
craft knife or other sharp blade to remove the base, leaving a
bottle with no bottom. The bottle will be turned upside-down
so the bottom becomes the plant pot and the top will become
the drainage hole.

Make three holes about 1cm (½-inch) down from the cut
edge. The holes will hold the string, so they need to be evenly
spaced. I found that heating a pointed skewer in a gas flame
for a few seconds was enough to penetrate and melt the plastic.

Cut three lengths of string – each around 30cm (12 inches) long – then thread one end into the hole from the outside inward and tie a knot at the end of the string inside the bottle and pull back through until the knot is held at the hole. Once all three pieces are secured to the bottle, tie them together at the very end – I then added an extra loop of string for hanging – but a metal ring would be better if you have one.

If the plastic bottle has a flip-top cap, cut this off using the sharp blade. If it has a screw top with a hole, keep this in place for drainage.

Use the marker pens to paint on a face, or in fact anything you like. Leave for an hour to dry then place a few stones or gravel into the end of the bottle, over the hole, to aid drainage, top off with compost, then repot your plant. Water freely as any excess will pour out of the hole at the bottom, then hang outside.

This is a great addition to a pot or patio garden, or place it just outside the back door to easily access fresh herbs.

PIGGY BANK – MONEY-SAVING UPCYCLE

This is a fun upcycle to do with the kids – the adults can do the cutting and the kids will love to glue, paint and save their pennies in a plastic piggy bank. A small, squat plastic bottle is ideal for this as all that is needed is a slot large enough to take coins into the side, but if you only have a larger bottle, just shorten it to make it 'piggy sized'.

Saved-up coins can be removed by unscrewing the snout. Try making cows and sheep, too, to live in a penny-saving farmyard!

You will need

1 x 300–400ml (10–14fl oz) single-use plastic bottle
scissors and craft knife
strong fast-acting glue
pot of eco-friendly pink paint suitable for plastic (chalk paints are good)
paintbrush
2 used wine corks
pins
pink felt pads, for the ears
skewer
wire or pipe cleaner, for the tail
multi-surface permanent marker pens, for eyes and snout

Start by cutting the cleaned bottle halfway down. I made a starter hole using a sharp blade then use scissors to cut along the circumference. Cut a slot large enough to take coins in the bottom half of the bottle.

Ease the top edge of the bottle inside the bottom of the bottle to shorten it and make a pig body shape, and check to make sure the slot is long enough by testing using a coin. The two halves can be kept in place with a spot or two of glue.

Once the slot and the bottle are firm, then the plastic can be painted pink. Hand-painting will work well, and to make the job less messy I took the cap off and stood the upturned bottle onto a stick outside while my granddaughter hand-painted (rather messily) when the air was still. Paint the cap too.

When all is dry, cut two corks on the diagonal and hand-paint all four pieces with pink paint. These will to be glued to the side of the bottle to make the legs.

I used pins stuck into the corks to make handling and painting them easy.

Cut diamond shapes from pink felt and after making two holes in the bottle for ears using a hot skewer, glue the ears in place. A curly tail can be made using thick wire or pipe cleaner painted pink once in place. The finishing touches of painting eyes and snout make this the most fun, useable, upcycled money saver ever!

BIRD FEEDER

Hanging bird feeders are so entertaining to watch; they will encourage birds to visit your garden or outdoor space and even to nest nearby. We have lots of visitors but the funniest ones are a family of blue tits that nest every year. We have screwed a bird box onto the shed above the door, and even though I am in and out of the shed several times a day, the birds are not put off. The reason for this, I believe, is that everything is handy – they have chosen a house close to all amenities. The bird feeder is about three feet away, the bird bath 6 feet away, a tree less than 4 feet away, so everything you need for a growing family (food, water, shelter and somewhere to hide) is literally on the doorstep. They probably brag to their friends that they don't need to travel at all – they work from home!

One bird feeder isn't enough for me because I like to attract different species. Goldfinches love sunflower seeds, whereas blue tits, sparrows, robins and finches seem to prefer mixed seeds. Bird feeders can work out to be quite expensive – I have paid around £40 in the past for a metal, squirrel-proof, rain-protected hanging feeder. Once in place and while watching the birds happily feeding from it, I realized I could probably recreate something similar using items I was about to throw away. I made it and it works!

It's a year on from making my first DIY bird feeder and it is still hanging proudly in place. The expensive store-bought alternative has long since irreparably broken.

You will need

1 litre (34fl oz) clear plastic bottle with cap
1 screwtop lid from a jam jar (or similar)
strong fast-acting glue
multi-surface permanent marker pen
a metal skewer or similar sharp-pointed object
a drill
2 plastic spoons
1 metal coat hanger
wire cutters or pliers
a clear plastic bowl (one of those single-use salad or trifle bowls
    works well – about 20cm/8 inches diameter)
wild bird seed
plastic funnel

Start by removing the screw cap from the bottle and glue it to the underside of the jam jar's screwtop lid. This will be used to screw back onto the bottle when the feeder is finished.

Use a marker pen to mark where the seed-dispensing holes are to be. Work with the bottle upside down, as that is how it will be used. Stagger four holes evenly around the bottle. Start with two about 7.5cm (3 inches) up from the screwtop and still part of the bottle neck. The next two space out and stagger up the bottle, finishing about 7.5cm (3 inches) down from the bottle's base.

Use then a hot skewer (heating the point on a gas flame), to make holes in the bottle where you have marked with pen. Once a hole has been made you will need to use a drill to gently widen the hole. These large holes will allow the seed to easily dispense. A drill will make a neat job of this rather than trying to make the hole bigger with the hot skewer.

Still working with the bottle in an upside-down position, use the hot skewer to make a slit below the drilled holes. These slits need to be about 2.5cm (1 inch) below the holes and wide enough to take the handle of a plastic spoon. Make a corresponding slit at the other side of the bottle to secure the handle. Slot the spoon through the bottle – positioning the cup of the spoon below the hole to become a perch for the bird while at the same time capturing seed as it is disturbed by the birds. Repeat with the other spoon on the other side.

Take the metal coat hanger, leave the hook at the top intact and bend down the shoulder parts, then cut off the straight pieces just after the bend. When I made my feeder I added the clear plastic bowl as an extra feature which helps to keep the seed in the spoons dry and I believe deters squirrels. Some would say it needs more than a plastic bowl to deter a squirrel but I swear

to you I have not seen one on it yet! I think the plastic bowl, because it wobbles when touched, puts off the sure-footed squirrel.

Make two holes in the top of the feeder (the bottom of the bottle) and pop in the two bends of the coat hanger. Make a hole in the base of the plastic bowl, invert and feed it down via the hook, securing it around the part where the two wires secure the coat hanger.

The feeder can now be filled with bird seed and to ensure none is lost when filling, I use a funnel. Once the bottle is filled, secure with the screw top (now firmly stuck to the jam jar lid), which will also catch seed and hang upside down. Suspend in a place where you can watch your upcycled single-use plastic actually benefiting nature.

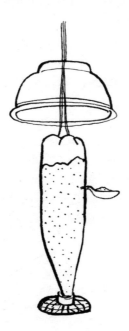

TWO-MINUTE SUPERSAVER – BATTERIES

I have included this little tip because once you get into the habit you will discover that those battery operated appliances that are seldom used will rarely need a new battery.

My example is my battery-operated temperature probe. I use it to test internal cooked or baked temperatures – handy to have, and I wouldn't be without it, but do I use it often? No. It has a metal probe that is inserted into the food, on a long wire that is clipped into a battery operated housing that has an alarm and temperature display. It is powered by two batteries.

The kitchen thermometer, even though it is switched off is still using the battery because the little view screen shows remaining battery life in the top corner. As I use this probe maybe only two or three times a year my habit is to simply lift one of the batteries from the housing, thereby disconnecting the power source, before placing back into the drawer. The battery is only slightly upended in the housing, it doesn't get lost, is quickly pushed back into place before the next use. I bought this probe thermometer when practising for *Bake Off* back in 2014 and am still on my original batteries.

Think about your seldom-used battery gadgets – my alarm clock in the spare bedroom gets the same treatment. Batteries do lose their charge over time but mine is still going strong.

CLOTHING

I have a wardrobe full of clothes I am sure I will never wear again. Charity shops do an excellent job of recycling and finding a new home for the once-worn glittery ball gown or the gentleman's trousers and jacket but everyday items can be harder to shift so it's best to prolong the life of wardrobe staples as much as possible.

I was so hard up back in the 1970s that I used to turn collars on shirts! It had been done by many during the war years. My grandmother used to do it to my grandad's shirts and they would then be worn as working shirts. Can you believe he used to wear a shirt and tie and he was a plumber? Later, when the shirts had finally had given up, she used to remove every button and cut the shirt into cleaning rags.

It is no fun being strapped for cash, but if money had never been a constraint I wouldn't be able to do half of the things I can do now.

Turn a Collar on a Shirt

There will be those favourite shirts or blouses that, had it not been for the collar, would still be very wearable. Problem is there is fraying and wear along the collar line. This is such a rewarding piece of 'cut and paste', and a brand-new-looking garment can be achieved in little more than an hour.

The collar will be attached to the shirt via a collar band and, using a very small pair of scissors or stitch unpicker, the worn section of the collar can be unpicked from the band. Once separated, simply flip it around and insert back into the band. A sewing machine will give a perfect professional finish, though neat hand-sewing works too.

I have removed a very large, dated '80s collar with sequins (oh my goodness, I used to love it) from a blouse, making it into a white cotton, grandad-collar shirt, which I now love and wear regularly.

Dirty Job Cloths

There are some clothing items that are either so well worn or split or torn that they will never be worn again and could never be passed on to a charity shop.

This is usually how clothing leaves my house, but rather than tipping it into the general waste bin, which will ensure it will end its life in landfill, I give everything a good final once-over.

First, I remove any buttons and zips and pop them into my sewing box – they always come in handy. I then cut the fabric into 20-cm (8-inch) squares and pop them onto a shelf in the utility room. When I want to treat my leather sofa, polish shoes or brass, or clean something really mucky I can reach for one of these cloths then discard it afterwards. I save my best cleaning cloths, which are used over and over, for non-oily or dirty jobs.

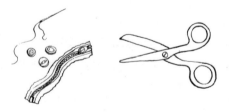

SOAP

Soap – bars of soap (not the liquid poured into plastic pump dispensers) can be upcycled easily and no one would ever know. My grandad used to save slivers of soap then boil them together, pour into a tin lid and reuse them as 'working soap' to clean his oily hands. Let us fast forward this idea to the twenty-first century and make it part of our mission to waste less and make best use of everything we have.

I have an attractive jar that I keep on the bathroom shelf, and when the bar of soap is what I best describe as a 'thin sliver', I pop it into the jar. Once the jar is full and when my grandchildren come around, we get to work. Any dressmaker readers can save the thinnest sliver and use as tailor's chalk.

Upcycled Soap Bars

You will need

food processor or fine grater
heatproof bowl
small saucepan
silicone moulds
plastic spatula and small-angled palette knife
small organza drawstring bags
slivers of used soap (you can include bars of single-use soap from hotels)
organic essential oil– a few drops of your scent of choice
soap or food colouring – a few drops

These are great little gift ideas to use as drawer fresheners or a new bar of soap. Children love making these. Grate the slivers to a powder using a food processor or fine grater then put them into a heatproof bowl. Set the bowl over a pan of barely simmering water, which will give sufficient heat to melt the soap. I add 2–3 tablespoons of hot water and stir until the soap gratings dissolve and the mixture is thick and smooth. More water may be required, it really depends on the soap.

I add a few drops of organic essential oil – ylang-ylang or lily of the valley are great for this as they have a gorgeous flowery perfume. Add one or two drops of food or soap colouring, give a stir to thoroughly combine, then transfer to silicone moulds.

I have mini heart moulds, I think they were originally bought for moulding chocolate but they are perfect for this. Force the thick soap into the mould using a small spatula then smooth off with a small-angled palette knife. Leave to firm up and set completely – usually takes an hour or so, longer for larger bars of soap.

Pop the soaps out of the moulds then put two or three into small organza pouches to give as small gifts, to perfume and line drawers or to hang in wardrobes. Alternatively, use much larger moulds and make brand new soap bars. Presented in a home-made gift box (see page 207), they make the perfect recycled gift.

Almost Free Liquid Soap

MAKES 500ML

You will need:

food processor or hand blender
Medium-sized mixing bowl

500ml (18fl oz) pump soap dispenser and funnel
60g (2oz) used soap slivers
380ml (13fl oz) boiling water
20ml (¾ oz) vegetable glycerine
50g (2oz) bicarbonate of soda
5–10 drops of essential oil of choice for perfume
2–3 drops of soap or food colour (optional)

This recipe excited me so much when I worked it out even though it took many attempts to get it just right. You can make 500ml liquid hand soap nearly for free. Hang onto your plastic or glass soap dispenser bottle as you will never need to buy liquid hand soap again.

Break the pieces of soap into smaller pieces by hand then either pop in a food processor or into a mixing bowl and blitz to a powder with a hand blender.

Pour in the freshly boiled water and add the glycerine, bicarbonate of soda and essential oil. As the bicarbonate of soda is added it will fizz a little but that is fine. Blitz again to ensure a smooth soap without any lumps then add the food colour, if using, and stir well. Add more water if the mixture is too thick.

Leave the soap to cool to room temperature, stirring from time to time to prevent the mixture separating.

Once cooled and the colour and perfume is to your liking transfer to the soap dispenser.

I got so carried away I created bottles of all colours. I might have to give some away as gifts!

REFILL NOT LANDFILL

I decided to include this little cleaning tip as I know many readers now favour refill shops to save on single-use plastic packaging. I am fortunate to have an eco-friendly refill shop close to where I live, who take pride in their plastic-free and zero-waste business. One of my favourite purchases is rapeseed oil, which is sold in a glass bottle that can then be taken back to the shop to refill.

Unlike many liquids, oil is very stubborn when it comes to leaving the inside of a bottle. I have to say I didn't ever give it a second thought when I used to throw my empty glass or plastic oil bottles into the bin until I read around contaminated recycling. Unless our items are thoroughly washed before being placed into the appropriate bin they will probably end up in landfill. Food residue on plastic is a 'no-no', and those in the business apparently refer to it as Aspirational Recycling – we say we're doing it but unless we clean the container it may not end up where we hope and expect it to go.

It may be worth checking with your local services to find out their rules. Aluminium drinks cans in some areas, for example, can be recycled without rinsing.

Cleaning the inside of oil bottles, cans and containers can be carried out effectively and quickly using a few simple ingredients.

The addition of coarse salt flakes in this mix here does two things – firstly it acts as a mild abrasive to help clean the inside of the bottle, and I read that salt also increases the oxidation of fatty acids, which causes the oil to break down. Washing soda is great at cutting through grease, as is soap and hot water. Your bottle will be as sparkling as new.

Deep Clean Your Bottles

MAKES 1 LITRE (34FL OZ)

You will need

  funnel
  1 litre (34fl oz) glass or plastic bottle with lid
  2 tbsp washing soda (sodium carbonate)
  5 drops eco-friendly washing-up liquid
  2 tbsp coarse salt flakes
  3–4 tbsp hot water, plus more to fill
  1 tsp bicarbonate of soda (to remove sticky label)

Place the funnel into the neck of the bottle and add all of the ingredients. Screw on the cap and give a good shake – a really good shake – for several minutes. Remove the cap then fill the bottle to the neck with hot water, replace the cap and leave for an hour, or longer if you can. During this time the natural chemicals will do their job of breaking down the fat, the salt will dissolve too and the whole lot can be poured down the sink.

A quick rinse with water and your bottle is as clean as a whistle and ready for the refill shop.

If there are sticky label residues or glue present on the outside of the bottle, this can be rubbed off easily using a dampened finger and a teaspoon of bicarbonate of soda.

WOODEN BRUSHES

Sweeping, scrubbing, vegetable, clothes, makeup and tooth-brushes are often plastic these days and little concern needs to be given to their care. When the bristles wear out or the brush looks shabby it is tossed away to end up in landfill and a new shiny one replaces it.

As my brushes wear out I am going back to basics and replacing them with wooden equivalents – yes, I now even have a wooden hairbrush and a bamboo toothbrush!

Wooden brushes need a little more care and attention than plastic, but they will last longer in the end. Back in the day, my brushes were always wooden, yet the handle could be replaced

and so could the head – so they lasted literally years and years. Those brushes that are in water a lot will dry out; a rub over with a smear of coconut oil will replenish and nurture the wood and at the same time add a water-resistant coating, ensuring they always stay in the best condition.

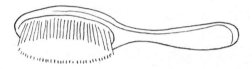

One golden rule is to always dry a wooden brush with the bristles facing downwards so that water can run off and not soak the base of the bristle, causing mould, odour and eventually rot. Wooden sweeping and household brushes tend to have a hole at one end of the handle for hanging, so don't be tempted to stand a wooden sweeping brush with bristles upwards to dry.

TIME FOR CRAFT
AND CREATION

As Christmas, or indeed any holiday season approaches, the shops, magazines and TV inundate us with celebrity endorsed products that will ensure we have the best holiday season ever if we buy this or that. I used to fall for it every time . . .

I can recall one Christmas, back in the 1990s, when I decided my Christmas tree had to be 'themed' and would be decorated only in red and silver. I had seen this on the cover of a magazine and considered I must be missing out on something and needed to up my game if I was to have the best Christmas, and one similar to this fantastic cover shoot. It cost me a small fortune and – knowing what I know now – those shots are taken many months before Christmas, everything is staged, the lighting is perfect and the snow outside is not real!

Take a deep breath, smile and have the confidence in knowing that Christmas is what you and your family do. It isn't what you *think* others do. Don't feel pressured into spending hard-earned cash on frills.

Christmas when children are small is priceless and I'm so lucky that I have a paper angel made for me by one of my grandchildren that comes out year after year. It has its own little storage box so it doesn't get crushed amongst other tree decorations, and although it is only a piece of paper, I love it. I treasure it above all of the new creations that are seemingly 'on trend' and must-buys in the shops every year.

Paper angels are so easy to make. Our local church decorated a whole tree with them one year and with only a set of white lights to illuminate them it was probably one of the most heart-warming Christmas trees I have ever seen. I promise that if you or the children gift a paper angel to someone at Christmas, it will be treasured.

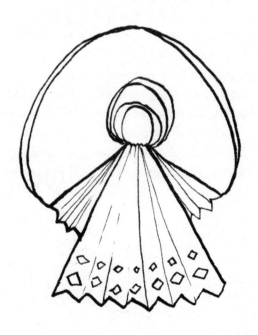

TWO-MINUTE SUPERSAVER –
SCISSOR SHARPENER

Crafting with paper using your best scissors, especially pinking shears, will blunt them. For an instant sharpen, simply take a piece of aluminium foil about 30cm (12 inches) square then fold it so that you have around 8–10 thicknesses. Use your blunt scissors to cut the foil over and over – cut thin strips until the scissors close and you will have sharpened them – both blades, both sides – quickly, easily and cheaply. As the foil hasn't been contaminated by food it can be popped into the metal recycling bin.

If you don't have foil to hand, fine sandpaper works a treat too – even if it has been used already. Fold a piece of used sandpaper, measuring between 15cm (6 inches) to 20cm (8 inches) square, in half with the rough sides facing outwards and cut into thin strips, same as with the foil, closing the blades together. After sharpening, wipe the blades of the scissors with a clean cloth.

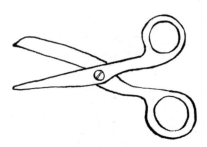

PAPER ANGELS

You will need

15cm (6 inch) square of white paper
scissors
paper glue
paper clip
silver or gold wrapping ribbon for halo and hanging

Make a series of small concertina folds in the paper from top to bottom. Open out slightly, then midway across the folds cut to just below halfway down with the scissors. Fold the cut flaps over and glue to the top of the body, securing with a paper clip until dried.

Use the scissors to cut tiny 'vs' in the folds, which when opened out give a beautiful lacy effect. The more tiny vs the better!

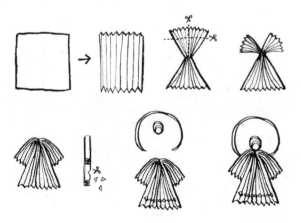

Open out and you will have created a simple angel form with wings and skirt. To add a hanger, glue a length of Christmas wrapping twine under the wings. For a head, create a double circle of wrapping twine and secure to the top.

Children's parties now boast a whole range of single-use plastic. I have made strings of colourful paper dolls strung around like bunting to decorate a party room or table, and even used edible rice paper, tinting them here and there with edible food colour, to continue the theme, and also set them as a cake collar.

A string of paper dolls is fun to make, the children can get involved and colour them in and even make it one of the party games. To make eight paper dolls you need only a sheet of A4 paper. Fold the sheet of paper in half lengthways and cut into two strips. Fold each strip into three, as a zig-zag rather than folding in either end. Draw a half doll alongside the fold, making sure the hands (the joining part) reach the fold at the other side of the paper. Cut around the figure and carefully open out. Repeat and join together at the hands with glue to create bunting or a chain.

PAINTING POTS

This is a great craft for adults and children. How often have you trailed the aisles in supermarkets and garden centres when it comes to Easter, Mother's Day or Christmas looking for a gift idea? Cut flowers are expensive and have come from goodness knows where; potted plants, too, are wrapped attractively in brightly coloured plastic packaging and bows to make them look bigger than they are.

I bought a tray of acrylic paints that cost not much more than a box of felt-tipped pens. The pack included just 12 colours in small pots – a paintbrush was included too. I had great fun painting three small terracotta pots that I had cleaned up. I painted on the simplest of flowers to make them look that bit special, then planted cuttings in them. Now they sit on my windowsill, side by side.

It got me thinking that this is a great craft for children and who wouldn't adore a rosemary cutting in a hand-painted pot as a birthday, Mother's Day, Christmas or Easter gift? A few spring-flowering bulbs planted in the autumn in hand-painted pots (terracotta or plastic) make a perfect Christmas gift, too.

A pot containing a small lavender plant will set you back a few pounds in the garden centre, yet a cleaned-up, home-painted pot containing a small healthy lavender cutting from your own mature plant will make an even better gift. (See notes on taking cuttings, page 293.)

DECORATED EGGS

I used to use scraps of silk fabric and Grandad's old silk ties to create the most amazing decorations on white eggs, which were used as Easter decorations. However, the dyes used in the fabrics made the eggs inedible and only suitable as a keepsake for a week or two. So I have been working on more sustainable methods of creating Easter treats that can be safely eaten and therefore not wasteful on food or energy.

Natural egg dyeing is appealing as an Easter craft; the patterns are natural and gorgeous and the eggs, after having been used for the Easter egg hunt, can be safely eaten – though my grandchildren tend to want to hold onto them as souvenirs.

You will need

old pair of tights
scissors
string or metal ties
large saucepan or 2 medium saucepans
4 tbsp white vinegar
liquid edible food or soap colours
spoon, whisk and tongs
edible flowers or leaves
6 white eggs
vegetable, sunflower, rapeseed or olive oil, for rubbing

Cut the tights into six lengths, each long enough to enclose an egg, about 15–20cm (6–8 inches). I find it easier to secure one of the open ends of the tights with a piece of string – forming an open bag. Once you've made six, set them aside.

Decide how many colours are to be made – let's say two. Fill two saucepans large enough to each hold three eggs around two-thirds full with cold water then add 2 tablespoons of white vinegar to each one. Add then several drops of chosen food colour – I used six drops, the colour needs to be strong – then stir with a small spoon or whisk.

Forage for flat, interesting edible foliage or flowers. In the springtime, daisies, forget-me-nots, wild garlic flowers and primroses are young, small and detailed and will transfer beautifully. Remove an egg from the water and secure the 'right side' of the flower or leaf to the egg. The underside of leaves tend to be concave, whereas the darker 'right side' is not. Using a primrose as an example, place the flower face next to the egg. This is surprisingly easy to do – I found the leaves and flowers didn't slip around if the shell has first been dampened lightly with water. Once the egg has its greenery or flowers attached, then insert it carefully into the little bag, which has already

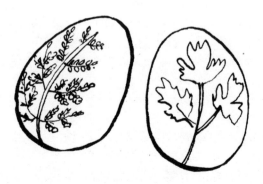

been secured at one end. Tighten and stretch the piece of nylon using the hands to secure the flowers to the egg, then tie off with another metal tie or length of string. The nylon needs to be taut so that the flowers are unable to move during the cooking of the egg. Do the same with the remaining eggs.

Place 3 eggs in each pan, each containing a different colour then bring to the boil and simmer for 15 minutes. Leave the eggs to cool slightly in the pan then use tongs to lift out onto a plate. Once completely cold, remove the nylon, flowers and leaves and admire the colour and patterns. Once completely cold, for a shiny finish rub them lightly with oil. These eggs are completely edible, brilliant for Easter celebrations and you are upcycling a pair of old tights!

DRYING FLOWERS

Dried flowers make me think about Victorian ladies sitting drinking tea and chatting, reading, doing their embroidery and generally passing away their afternoon time. I am not talking huge dried-flower arrangements, I mean dainty posies wrapped in twine or paper ribbon and given as gifts or keepsakes or a small, hanging, perfumed pomander.

There are certain flowers that dry to look better than others. Cornflowers, for example, make excellent dried flowers because their colour is preserved as well as their shape. Other flowers dry well, too, and I have been experimenting with various wild flowers. Buttercups are lovely and a tiny posy taped to a birthday gift is enchanting. (See page 209 about eco gift wrapping – I have stopped using shiny paper, wrapping tape, bows and the like.) I discovered when trying to dry large rose blooms that they dropped their petals during the process. But they didn't go to waste – see page 118 for how to create rose petal confetti and scented pot pourri instead.

Other flowers that have dried well for me are rose buds and blooms, aquilegia, philadelphus, lisianthus and peonies. Add a few dried poppy seed heads and you have the makings of something beautiful that will last and last. Use fresh garden flowers, wild flowers or some from a bouquet before they start to fade.

You will need

fresh flowers for drying
string
hooks

paper florist tape

dry, warm dark place – I use my airing cupboard

Pick the flowers in the morning when the weather is cool and dry. Tie the flowers with string in small bunches of no more than about six for small flowers and singly for large blooms such as peonies.

Hang them upside-down from a hook in a dry warm dark place such as an airing cupboard. Check them from time to time, but after 10 days to two weeks the flowers will have dried in their open state with their colour intact. Remove any small leaves that have died and may spoil their appearance, trim the stalks then wrap paper florist tape around them to secure.

This method can also be used to preserve a treasured bouquet of flowers from someone special or to always be reminded of a special event. Rather than leave the flowers in water until they fade and die, while they still look quite fresh, tie them with string at the stems and hang them upside-down in a dark, warm place. Once dried, after around two weeks, the colours may be faded and the green leaves may turn a little brown, but your precious collection of blooms will have been lovingly preserved.

I picked up a small wicker frame around 25cm (10 inches) in diameter for a couple of pounds and secured my selection of dried flowers using florist wire, added the dried poppy seed heads, a few drops of essential oil directly onto the flowers, then hung it on the bathroom door to provide me with the most beautiful perfumed pomander – with no plastic involved.

PRESSED FLOWERS

The first time I ever pressed flowers was as part of a school project when we were tasked to make a bookmark – oh dear, that is more than fifty years ago!

Bringing this craft into the twenty-first century, I now get the finest pleasure from a display of pressed summer flowers – having retained their vibrant colours – in a glass frame to please me during the dreary winter days. It is so easy to do. I bought four small, glass frames and decided to display the 'four seasons' – it really is gorgeous. I gave one frame to a friend as a birthday gift, choosing flowers of blues and purples as I knew she had recently redecorated a room with this colour scheme.

You will need

an open basket or bowl for collecting the flowers (dropping them into a bag can damage the petals)
scissors
2 sheets of greaseproof, baking or brown packaging paper
thick heavy book
small rolling pin
blunt knife or tweezers
glass display frame
paper glue or edible glue (see below)

Choose your flowers when the weather is dry and they are at their prime – no browning or missing petals. I find flat-faced flowers press very successfully – cosmos, daisies and cornflowers – whereas flowers with lots of petals such as roses are reluctant to lie flat.

Cut with scissors, lay in a basket or bowl, being careful not to bruise them, then take two sheets of greaseproof paper and your thickest book – about 10cm (4 inches) thick; I use a very thick French dictionary. Open out in the middle then lay over one sheet of the paper. Lay the flowers in a single layer onto the paper then scrunch up the second sheet and lay it over them, flattening any lumpy centres or buds carefully before pressing with a small rolling pin. I have found scrunching the paper helps keep the flowers in place when closing the book.

Make sure none of the flowers are touching each other, they need a small amount of space, and carefully close the book and set to one side, weighing it down with more books, if you have them, and forget about it for two weeks.

Take the flowers from the book and very carefully peel back the paper, easing any pressed petals away from the top sheet using a blunt knife or tweezers. Decide how you want to display the flowers, and lay them out on the frame backing. A few drops of simple paper glue will work well to stick the flowers in place; I use the glue very sparingly, just a drop here and there. I sometimes use edible glue, which is a simple sugar and water gel, to adhere the flowers to the glass. Close the frame and enjoy.

I hope you enjoy pressing flowers as much as I do. I love the creative possibilities surrounding these preserved beauties. You can use them to make personalized birthday cards, gift tags and I have seen them adhered to attractive stones and pebbles, varnished and used as paperweights.

DRYING LAVENDER

If you have a garden and don't already have a lavender plant or two, it is well worth finding a place for it. Lavender grows in just about any soil, doesn't suffer drought and during June and July will give you an abundance of purple or white flowers clustered together on long stems. The fragrance is unforgettable and can be captured forever by drying. The health benefits of lavender are well-documented and I really must try to do more with mine.

Lavender will grow well in a pot on a patio and will not need much care. A new lavender plant will retain its gorgeousness for two years, but then you will notice the stems thicken, the flowers are fewer and you may think it has had its day. Lavender benefits from an annual prune and this should be done in August when the flowers have faded. Cut back fairly strictly down to a shoot, and before the frosts come you will see your lavender has started to sprout again. I had a row of lavender that was very old and woody through lack of pruning but before digging it out to start again I decided 'kill or cure' was the way forward, and at the end of August I cut the plants down to just a few inches above the ground. There was no green to be seen. However, nature is a miracle worker and in a few weeks the tiniest green sprigs appeared from the thick woody base, to be followed by a thick healthy green display the following spring and an abundance of flowers in June.

Lavender is also easy to raise from cuttings (see page 293), so even if you don't have a plant yet, I am sure a friend or neighbour will let you take cuttings from theirs.

Back to drying lavender. Pick the flowers just as they are beginning to fade and when the bees have stopped enjoying them. It is useful to save paper bags as these are the perfect vessels for storing the stems. Drop the fading blooms into the bags as you cut them and leave them in a warm dry place with the bag open. From time to time I shake the bag to help loosen the drying seeds. Once I have a bag of loose faded blooms and seeds I transfer them into an air-tight box to use as I need them. I have made lavender bags in June using the dried blooms from the previous year – they have a long shelf life! Turn to page 214 to read about how to make lavender bags as gifts, which as well as adding a natural perfume to your car, drawers and wardrobes will also deter moths and other insects.

Lavender is edible and a few fresh flowers make adorable edible cake decorations – I like to pair them up with large, star-shaped, bright yellow cucumber flowers and feathery green from fennel. This edible posy on a cake is breathtaking.

TIP: A bunch of spent lavender flowers scattered around the floor of my chicken housing deters pests, particularly red mite, at a time when they are most active.

ROSE PETALS

If you have a rose garden and want to continue to enjoy the beauty of different-coloured rose petals even in the winter months or if you are planning a wedding and want to make your own eco-friendly biodegradable confetti, this tip is a great one. Drying rose petals is easy and I have had such fun displaying bowls of scented pot pourri, as well as creating paper bags of confetti and scented rose petals to make superb mini gifts. Try this with other flowers, too – a bought bouquet can be upcycled just as it starts to fade, to provide scented bowls of colourful loveliness around the house.

You will need

rose petals
basket or large bowl
newspaper
warm dark room
essential oils for scent (optional)

Harvesting petals for drying has to be done at just the right time. Choose a still day when the roses are dry. Select a full bloom before it drops its petals – the correct time is when you cup a hand around a bloom and gently squeeze it and it releases all of the petals into the palm. If the rose resists, leave it a little longer. Have to hand a basket or large bowl to drop the delicate petals into. After collecting, bring the petals inside and lay out sheets of newspaper either on a floor or table in a room that is dry and fairly dark.

Laying out the petals in a warm yet dark environment dries them quickly and preserves their colour. Drying fully will take around a week to ten days. Move the petals around from time to time until they feel quite crisp and obviously dried. They are ready when you can run your hands through them without any sticking to your fingers. Transfer to paper bags to store until required.

A drop or two of your favourite essential oil added to the bag of petals will provide a subtle perfume, too.

DRYING HYDRANGEA HEADS

I have two well-established hydrangea bushes in my garden which are covered in dark-pink blooms in July and August. As the late summer turns into autumn, the colours change to a variety of pale, dusky pinks through to dark slate blue – I love them. I started drying them many years ago using various methods. Some say to hang the blooms upside-down in a dark place, others to dry upright indoors in a vase without water, others suggest drying in water with sugar added, but I have found this method below is the one that works best for me.

You will need

hydrangea blooms
secateurs
large vases or water containers
dark, well-ventilated, cool yet frost-free place
water
2–3 tbsp vegetable glycerine

I have found that the best results are obtained by cutting the blooms at exactly the right time. Too early and the flowers simply die, too late and the colours have faded so much that each one looks the same, a kind of off-white, brown around the edges and maybe frost damaged.

I have cut blooms in late August and early September (in the UK). The flower colours are perfect but alas the timing is wrong. After a week or so the petals had shrivelled and died, even in water. My best results have come from blooms collected towards the end of September and in early October. The colours are good, not vibrant as in the summer but instead an array of subtle dusky pinks, creams, greys and blues.

Choose a day when the blooms are dry and cut a long stem of at least 30cm (12 inches) using secateurs, cutting just above a leaf node or set of leaves. This will ensure the bush flowers next year. Carefully remove the leaves from the cut stems by gently pulling them off in a downwards direction, then place in a large vase filled with about 7.5cm (3 inches) of cold water with 2–3 tablespoons of vegetable glycerine. Place the blooms away from direct light. I keep mine in the garage – it is dark, frost-free and I can easily pop in from time to time to check on them.

Don't be tempted to crowd the vase – the blooms need space so that air can freely circulate around them and they can dry evenly. In a large vase that would normally comfortably hold a large bouquet, I add only four heads.

The hydrangeas can now be left for several weeks – they can take around 4–6 weeks to dry completely, depending on temperature and other conditions. They will drink the water as they die down naturally in their own time. After the drying time and when the water has all gone, the petals will feel dry yet soft and firm. I have found that the addition of the glycerine prevents the petals becoming too papery and fragile. The blooms can now be used and displayed in vases or stored until Christmas to use in festive decorations. One year I filled a huge basket with them and stood it in a fireplace – I enjoyed them for months and months.

If you don't grow hydrangeas yourself, ask your neighbours if they have hydrangeas in the garden and are not doing anything with them, as they might be only too pleased for you to prune them. Or if you have been gifted some hydrangeas in a bouquet or display, I would certainly dry them as above, rather than transfer them to the compost bin.

BIODEGRADABLE CHRISTMAS WREATH

I have made a 100 per cent biodegradable Christmas wreath for several years now and each one is much better than the year previous. This is extremely popular with my social media audience, so I thought it needed a mention in this book.

I love decorating the house at Christmas and most of the treasures have been with me for decades, so they bring back great memories as they are hung and adorned in similar places each year. I used to have a reusable Christmas wreath that, looking back, was so tacky – with its plastic holly, berries and bows – that it was confined to landfill some five years ago.

Had I realized then the problems we were soon to face with our planet, I think I might have tried to repurpose it in some way. However, what's done is done, and moving on my annual Christmas wreaths of the future have been – and will always be – totally biodegradable and once the season has faded are simply dropped onto the compost heap. This means, of course, no glitter, no glue, no wires, plastic or foam can be used in making these wreaths. So if you have access to greenery, this is a fun, inexpensive and easy project.

You will need

4 holly branches with long bendy stems (about 1–1.25m/
   3–4 feet)
4–6 shorter holly, ivy or other evergreen stems with leaves
garden gloves
secateurs

jute twine or green wool
dried hydrangea heads
dried fruits (such as orange slices)
cinnamon sticks
rose hips
large laurel leaves
fern leaves
pine cones
feathers

Start by making a frame. Forage for long, bendy branches – when I say 'bendy' I mean a long length of 1–1.25m (3–4 feet) that can be formed into a hoop without cracking, splitting or breaking. Holly branches are perfect for this and I am fortunate to be able to access long lengths from my garden.

I cut 3–4 such lengths to form the frame for the wreath. The first two lengths can be curled into a fairly uneven circle and joined together using wool or biodegradable twine then the other two lengths can be twisted around the joins and the rest of the hoop to reinforce it. Once the hoop has some stability from the four branches, intertwine a few smaller holly, ivy or any evergreen branches with leaves through the original frame, securing as you go with wool or twine.

The project soon starts to take shape, gaining strength as you thicken it out by wrapping round more stems with leaves. I have found that the thicker the original frame, the better the finished result. Once the frame is sturdy I tie in dried hydrangea flower heads all around, then at around '5 o'clock' on the wreath I set a posy of dried fruit slices and cinnamon sticks with rosehips tied into a huge bunch, surrounded by large laurel leaves, fern leaves, pine cones and feathers, giving a beautiful effect.

When you are happy, add a hanging piece of twine and admire your eco-friendly craft. The colours are simply beautiful and if made 2–3 weeks before Christmas will continue to look resplendent into the New Year and beyond.

TIME TO BAKE

When the number of jobs to do around the house and garden stack up and I wonder when I'll fit in my favourite pastime I often turn to my collection of 'easy' favourites that I know off by heart, because I know the family love them and they can be done in a jiffy.

I have included a number of these baking recipes that can be made effortlessly, needing little or no kit, and each cuts down on process without cutting out flavour, texture or appearance. Baking has never been this easy. Whether you want to make a cake, biscuits, bread or pastry, a simple recipe awaits you. I have included a couple of recipes that will make excellent use of pastry offcuts, too.

The ingredients I use are always simple, affordable and accessible. Rather than reaching for the plastic packet of mass-produced baked goods, let's have some fun, know exactly what ingredients are being used and make our own treats.

The following recipes will not fail you even if you have never baked before.

FIGURING OUT HOW BIG YOUR TIN IS

You have a tin in the drawer, had it years or maybe it was given to you. It is a strange shape, so you've no idea what capacity it is and therefore no idea which recipe will suit it. It's fairly straightforward to fit cake tins to recipes, being 20 or 23cm (8 or 9 inches) in diameter or square. Loaf or Bundt-style tins, though, are not as easy, as you first need to work out what size they are.

To do this you will need a set of digital weighing scales. Place the empty tin onto the scales and reset to zero. Fill the tin to within about 2cm (¾ inch) of the top with water. The weight registered on the scales will indicate whether the tin is a 1lb (or 500g), 2lb (or 1kg). The weight of the water is roughly the capacity of the tin.

TIN SIZE CALCULATOR

How many times have you fancied a bit of baking? You see a mouthwatering cake photo in a magazine, have a read through and are delighted to know all the ingredients are in your cupboard. The tin size states 18cm (7 inches) round and yours is 20cm (8 inches), alternatively you have a 18cm (7-inch) square. Does it matter? Yes, unfortunately it does. A square tin needs more cake batter than a round one of the same size and a 18cm (7-inch) recipe baked in an 20cm (8-inch) tin will look as though it has failed to rise and will overbake if you follow the baking time in the recipe.

However, rather than go out to buy yet another piece of kit my Cake Tin Calculator will help you to scale up or down your ingredients to suit the tins that you have. There may seem to be lots of figures here, but let me explain.

Let us assume the recipe you want to use states you need a 20cm (8 inch) round tin but all you have is a 18cm (7 inch). Go to the section for 20cm (8 inch) – follow the column down to 18cm (7 inch) and see that the ingredients need to be multiplied by 0.8 to give a cake of the same depth.

So, 130g (4½oz) butter would become 104g (3½oz). But what about eggs? If the recipe stated 3 eggs and multiplied by 0.8 gives 2.4, I would add two eggs and 1 tablespoon of milk. Over 2.5, I would add an extra egg.

See the cake tin calculator table on pages 320–1.

LINING PASTE

Have you ever said to yourself, 'I would bake a cake but lining the tin with paper is what I find the most fiddly and time-consuming?' If so, lining paste is a life-changer and it has many uses. This paste is a must for Bundt tins, can be used instead of greasing for pastries, cupcakes, pudding basins – in fact, anything where a recipe asks you to grease or line the vessel.

Not only is it quick and easy to make, it keeps for weeks in the fridge, is cheaper than buying cake-release sprays, there is no packaging, no aerosol and no baking paper needed – and it works. Cakes and baked goods will simply fall out of their tins!

Take a few minutes to make a 300g (10oz) jar. It is vegan (if you make sure you use vegan shortening), and you can use gluten-free flour for a gluten-free version.

You will need

large mixing bowl
hand-held electric whisk
pretty jar with lid
100g (3½oz) vegetable shortening
100g (3½oz) flour (can replace with gluten-free)
100ml (3½fl oz) oil (I prefer vegetable or sunflower oil)

In a roomy mixing bowl, place the vegetable shortening then add the flour. Use the mixer to whisk until thick and smooth. With the mixer running on a slow speed, pour in the oil in a thin, steady stream until you have a smooth paste the consistency of double cream. Transfer to the jar, seal with the lid and keep in the fridge to use from chilled.

When ready to bake, brush the paste over your tin with a pastry brush, then add your cake batter.

TIP: When making dark-coloured cakes such as chocolate, ginger or fruit, try stirring 1 teaspoon of cocoa powder into 2 tablespoons of lining paste to make a dark paste.

NOTES: A lining paste can be made using butter, lard or margarine in place of the vegetable shortening, though the shelf life may be reduced. I have found a lining paste made using any of these fats will last up to two weeks only, so maybe make a smaller quantity if you are doing this.

To avoid contamination of lining paste I always take out a measure using a clean tablespoon straight into the tin then brush it around with a pastry brush rather than dipping in and out of the jar using the same brush. Any debris introduced into the paste could cause mould to form.

MERINGUES WITH LEMON CURD

This recipe will make use of any egg leftovers – whites for the meringues and yolks for lemon curd. Alternatively, make the whole recipe using just two eggs – no waste, no special kit, no piping and a fabulous colourful, naturally gluten-free dessert that so many love.

You can make the lemon curd at any time when you have leftover yolks and add to buttercreams to flavour them, stir into cream for a trifle topping, use in quick steamed puddings (see page 71) or simply on its own on fresh bread, toast or scones.

MAKES 6

You will need

2 large glass mixing bowls and 1 small
hand-held electric whisk
baking sheet lined with a sheet of baking parchment or
    greaseproof paper
wooden spoon or fork
spatula

FOR THE MERINGUE NESTS
2 egg whites
120g (4oz) caster sugar
½ tsp cornflour

FOR THE LEMON CURD CREAM
2 egg yolks
60g (2oz) sugar
40g (1½oz) butter
zest and juice of 1 lemon (or try ½ grapefruit, 2 limes or 2 passion fruit)
250ml (8fl oz) double or whipping cream

TO SERVE
fresh seasonal fruits and a dusting of icing sugar

You will need a large roomy mixing bowl that is clean and grease-free. Grease will impede the fluffing up of the egg whites and I find a glass bowl better than plastic for this reason – I think plastic can hold onto grease even after washing.

To make the meringues, place the egg whites into the bowl and whisk with a hand-held electric whisk to a soft, fluffy light mix that stands up in soft peaks when the whisk is taken out.

Add 1 large tablespoon of the sugar and whisk for 1 minute before adding the next spoonful. It should take about 5 or 6 spoonfuls to use up all of the sugar, then you can add the cornflour. The meringue will now be thick, shiny, smooth and glorious.

Turn the oven on to 130°C/250°F/gas ½. First, use a bit of the meringue left on the whisk to dab around the underside of the baking sheet to glue the paper in place so that it doesn't slip and slide around when the meringues are being shaped.

Take a tablespoon and divide the meringue into six piles onto the secured baking paper. Use the rounded end of the spoon to swirl the meringue into a rough nest shape about 10cm (4 inches) in diameter. Don't get hung up on perfection, just try to create a hollow in the middle of each blob.

Pop the sheet of meringues into the oven and bake for 50 minutes, then turn the oven off.

The perfect meringue for me needs to be crisp on the outside and just soft and marshmallowy on the inside. To check that your meringues are perfect, while they are still in the oven gently peel off one of the nests from the paper. The base should be dry and non-sticky. If still wet, leave in the oven for a further 20 minutes.

Once cooked, leave them in the oven but wedge the door open by slotting a wooden spoon in the gap to prevent it closing. Leaving the meringues to cool slowly will prevent them cracking.

To make the quick lemon curd, simply place the yolks, sugar, butter, lemon zest and juice in a small saucepan on a low heat and stir constantly for several minutes until the butter melts and the mix slowly thickens. Once bubbling, take from the heat and transfer to a cold bowl using the spatula. Alternatively, if you want to make a lemon curd any time from leftover yolks, follow the method here then transfer to a clean jar with a well-fitting lid and once cold store in the fridge for 2–3 weeks. (I've even used it after 4 weeks.)

When ready to assemble the meringues, peel from the paper then put back onto the baking paper.

Whisk the cream in a clean large roomy bowl until starting to thicken, but still a little sloppy. Take two spoonfuls of the cream and stir through the bowl of cold lemon curd. This just loosens the thick curd, making it easier to combine with the cream. Add the loosened lemon curd to the cream and stir through, not too thoroughly – I like to see a few lemon flashes in the filing. As the lemon curd is stirred into the cream the mix will thicken further, so stir long enough for the cream to drop thickly from the spoon.

Spoon into the crisp meringue nests then decorate with lots of colourful fresh fruits and a dusting of icing sugar. Dressing and decorating the nests on the baking paper will save on cleaning up. Any drops of cream and scatterings of icing sugar can be scrumpled up in the paper and discarded without messing up your worktop.

The meringues and lemon curd can be made days in advance. Store the meringues in an airtight tin and the lemon curd in a jar in the fridge and assemble the whole lot on the day you need them. These meringues will stay crisp after filling for 2–3 hours. A perfect low-stress dessert for entertaining.

VICTORIA SANDWICH CAKE

I have decided to include my basic Victoria sponge cake recipe in this book because for me it is often where baking starts. I started with this recipe, as did my children and grandchildren. It is easy, inexpensive and once perfected is the base for so many other recipes – the only difference being flavourings and quantities. Once you know it, this recipe can be adapted to use up lots of different odds and ends.

I describe below a traditional 'creaming method', which emphasizes the importance of incorporating air into the batter for a light, well-risen cake without the need for additional chemical raising agent (which I can always taste).

You will need

2 x 15cm (6-inch) loose-bottomed sandwich tins or see cake
   tin calculator on page 322 to adjust recipe to fit your tin
   base-lined with reusable baking parchment (see page 16) and
   brushed with lining paste (see page 131)
medium-sized mixing bowl
hand-held electric whisk
metal spoon
small spatula
125g (4½oz) any room-temperature butter or margarine (see
   home-blend on page 14)
1 tsp vanilla extract
125g (4½oz) caster sugar (see home-blend on page 21)
2 large eggs
125g (4½oz) self-raising flour (see home-blend on page 17)

TO DECORATE (OPTIONAL)
strawberry or raspberry jam
a dusting of icing sugar
whipped cream
fresh fruits

First, preheat the oven to 180°C/350°F/gas 4 and prepare the
tins. Then place the home-blend butter, vanilla and sugar in
the mixing bowl and whisk on high for several minutes until the
mix is creamy, pale and smooth.

Add the eggs one at a time, whisking well between each
addition. To avoid a curdle, start whisking the egg into the mix

in the same place – that is, don't be tempted to swirl the whisks around, keep the whisk in one place, increasing the speed until you can see that the mix has emulsified and is smooth. At this stage you can move the whisk around and incorporate the rest of the butter and sugar.

Once you have a smooth batter, sift over the flour and fold in with a large metal spoon. Use slow, full movements with the spoon. Imagine the bowl is a clock face – start at 12 o'clock and take the spoon all the way down to 6 o'clock, make a half turn of the bowl and repeat. Once the flour has been fully incorporated, take your time, don't rush the folding in as we need to hold on to all of that valuable air that was incorporated during the whisking. Once the batter is thick and smooth with no unmixed flour, divide between the two tins and bake in the oven for 18–20 minutes until risen, golden and firm to the touch.

Leave to cool in the tins for 10 minutes then turn out onto a cooling rack and leave to go completely cold – around half an hour. I run a blunt knife around the edges of the cake to release any adhered crumb once the tins are cool enough to handle.

The finest sponge will be evenly baked, with no brown crispy edges or cracked top, and will have a perfect presentation side. When I see a gorgeous Victoria sandwich cake with cooling ridges on the presentation sponge, it niggles me. Not a problem if the cake is going to be covered in buttercream, but left bare it should look beautiful and flawless.

Turning out the sponges to avoid cooling tray lines is quite easy. With your two sponges still in the tins, have a look and decide which one is the most evenly baked with the best colour – this will be the top (presentation) sponge, so set that tin to one side. Lay one side of the cooling rack over the sponge that will be the base sponge, then flip the tin and rack over. Ease the tin from the sponge, remove the base-lining parchment and leave to go cold.

The remaining sponge, still in its tin, now has to be turned out – but not directly onto the cooling rack as the metal will leave permanent marks. To avoid this, fold a clean tea towel into thirds lengthways and lay it over the top of the cool sponge. With the towel being held quite firmly in each hand and taut across the cake, flip it upside down so that the top of the cake is turned onto the towel and then put it face down onto a work surface. Let go of the towel, which is still under the sponge. Remove the tin and lining parchment then use the left hand to lift one end of the towel which will lift the sponge without damaging it. You can then use your right hand to support it underneath and carefully transfer onto the cooling tray, presentation side upwards. No ridges and a perfect-looking sponge.

This cake can be sandwiched together simply with strawberry or raspberry jam and finished with a dusting of icing sugar on the top, or filled with jam, cream, decorated with fresh fruits and made into a fabulous showstopper.

This very basic recipe will also make 12 mini cakes baked in paper cases in a 12-hole muffin tin, or the batter can be divided between the 12 holes of a muffin tin brushed with lining paste. I find an ice-cream scoop to be the perfect measure.

LEMON YOGHURT CAKE

When mixing a cake batter I usually adopt the creaming method (described in the previous recipe) using a hand-held electric whisk. This method was taught to me at school and involves beating the butter and sugar in a large, roomy bowl. We did it then with a wooden spoon, though nowadays an electric whisk is much easier. Once the mix was pale, smooth and fluffy, only then were the eggs beaten in and finally the flour was sifted over. At this stage we were taught to change over to a metal spoon and the batter was folded (stirred slowly) until smooth and gorgeous. Last of all, the flavourings were added.

I still mix cake batter this way. I am not a fan of table-top mixers for cake making, even though many recipes nowadays champion the 'all-in-one' method with additional raising agent to give the sponge more height. Unfortunately, I can taste raising agent if more than around 1.5 per cent baking powder to flour is used, so the traditional mixing method, incorporating maximum air, gives me the best cake.

However, when time is tight this little cake is perfect – all in the bowl together – and it makes excellent use of natural yoghurt. I need not use extra baking powder (raising agent) for a rise as the acidity in the yoghurt and lemon give an extra boost to the ingredients. It's a piece of cake!

Yoghurt does not freeze well – it tends to separate – so if my yoghurt is fast approaching its expiry date (and even if it has by a day or two) I use it rather than resign it to end of life in landfill.

This little cake is fast and no fuss and will avoid wasting your pot of unused dated yoghurt.

You will need

1 x 500g (1lb) loaf tin (see page 322) brushed with lining paste
   (see page 131)
medium-sized mixing bowl
hand-held electric whisk
spatula or wooden spoon
125g (4½oz) self-raising flour (see home-blended on page 17)
50g (2oz) caster sugar
40ml (1½fl oz) rapeseed or olive oil
1 egg
125ml (4fl oz) natural yoghurt
finely grated zest and juice of 1 lemon
1 tbsp caraway or poppy seeds

Preheat the oven to 160°C/325°F/gas 3 and prepare the loaf tin.

Place all of the ingredients into the mixing bowl then use the whisk to blend everything together until smooth – around 2 minutes.

Use the spatula or wooden spoon to transfer to the prepared tin then bake for 40 minutes until golden brown, well-risen and smelling gorgeous. Take out of the oven and leave in the tin set on the cooling tray.

Once cool enough to handle, take out of the tin and leave to go completely cold. This cake will keep up to a week in an airtight tin or plastic box.

LEMON AND YELLOW COURGETTE CAKE

This recipe is easy to make, dairy free and makes fantastic use of courgettes. If you grow your own you will know that once they start fruiting, they just keep going! Choose the youngest, small fruits for this recipe, before the seeds develop, as they are less watery.

This makes a moist, zingy, bright little traybake (or 16 muffins). I prefer yellow courgettes but if you have green ones try making a lime version.

You will need

20cm (8 inch) square loose-bottomed cake tin, base-lined and
    brushed with lining paste (see page 131) or 2 large muffin trays,
    lining 16 holes with paper cases or brushed with lining paste
large mixing bowls
250g (9oz) yellow or green courgettes
finely grated zest of 1 lemon (reserve the juice for the icing) or
    2 limes
1 tsp lemon extract
2 large or 3 medium eggs
190g (7oz) caster sugar
160ml (5fl oz) rapeseed, sunflower or vegetable oil
290g (10oz) self-raising flour(see home-blended on page 17)
50g (2oz) icing sugar
juice of the lemon or limes and extra zests or sprinkles to decorate

TIP: Wrap a foil collar around the outside of the tin to diffuse
the heat while baking, ensuring an even bake and a flat top.

Preheat the oven to 180°C/350°F/gas 4 and prepare the tin/s.

Start by grating the courgette into a large mixing bowl using a coarse grater, add the finely grated lemon zest and the lemon extract, give a stir and set aside.

In a second mixing bowl, whisk together the eggs and sugar until pale and increased in volume. Add the oil and whisk again, then sift over the flour and fold in with a large metal spoon. When everything is well combined add the bowl of grated courgettes, mix well, then transfer to the prepared tin.

Bake for 35–40 minutes until the cake is risen, golden and firm to the touch. Leave to cool in the tin set on a cooling rack. Turn out onto a square plate or board then remove the loose bottom from the tin. I often use the bottom as the presentation side for an even finish.

Once cold, mix a water icing. Simply add the juice of the zested lemon (or lime) to the sifted icing sugar to until the mix has the consistency of thick, smooth pouring cream. Add the juice to the icing sugar a spoon at a time, it will require less liquid than you might imagine. Pour this over the cooled cake and spread to the edges. Scatter over a few lemon zests or sprinkles.

Allow to set then cut into 12 slices.

TIP: To achieve clean-cut slices, pop the finished iced cake
into the freezer for about 20 minutes to firm up, then slice.

UNDEMANDING SEED BREAD

If you think that bread baking is not for you – no time to mix, knead, rise, shape, prove and bake – I fully understand. You need to set aside a good three hours to make a standard loaf; that doesn't mean you are unable to get on with other things, but it can still be tying.

I cannot tell you how many times I have jumped on my bike, gone down to the shops and back at a rate of knots before my 50 minutes' proving time is up! Soda breads are very quick but I am afraid it is not for me. I can taste the bicarbonate of soda and the keeping qualities are poor, as a loaf really needs to be eaten the same day.

This 'no-knead' bread recipe is great. All ingredients in the bowl together, a quick stir, leave overnight or longer, then bake. I have adapted a recipe passed to me several years ago by a follower from Norway and it is a real favourite, especially when I am not going to be at home to tend to bread making but still prefer home-baked. It keeps really well, uses less yeast than many home baking recipes and tastes amazing.

A great bread for the weekend. Mix the ingredients together early Friday evening and enjoy fresh bread at Saturday morning brunch. These ingredients will yield a family-sized loaf.

You will need

roomy mixing bowl

plastic spatula or large spoon

a solid casserole dish with a well-fitting lid – mine is cast-iron and
measures 18cm (7 inch) diameter, 9cm (3 inch) deep

a 15cm (6 inch) circle of reusable baking parchment in the base
(taken from my cake tins)

bench scraper

300g (10oz) white bread flour

50g (2oz) porridge oats

50g (2oz) mixed seeds

1 tsp salt

3g dried yeast

300ml (10fl oz) cold water

2 tsp sesame oil for the pot and extra porridge oats and seeds to
roll the dough in (about 2 tbsp)

Place all of the dry ingredients into the large mixing bowl,
pour over the cold water then using the spoon or spatula, stir
sufficiently only to combine the ingredients, making sure all of
the flour has absorbed the water. Place a plate over the bowl to
cover and leave on the work surface for a minimum of 8 hours
and up to 24.

The next day, oil the casserole dish. Pour 2 teaspoons of
sesame oil into the dish and use your hands to smear it around,
paying particular attention to the high sides. The sesame oil
gives a gorgeous nutty flavour to the crust. Lay the circle of
reusable baking parchment in the base. Place the cold casserole
dish in the oven and to a very high 250°C/500°F/gas 6.

While the oven is heating up, use the spatula or spoon to gently ease the risen fermented dough from the sides of the bowl. A thin-ended spatula is handy because its flexibility will neatly get down between the dough and the sides of the bowl and then it is easier to flip the dough from the sides of the bowl to the centre. Repeat four or five times so that a ball of shaggy sticky dough is sitting in the base of the bowl. Don't stress about trying to handle the dough like an artisan bread baker, the aim is simply to discharge all of the dough from the bowl onto the prepared work surface in a single lump.

Sprinkle 2 tablespoons or a good scattering of oats and seeds over the worktop and then, when the oven has reached temperature, remove the very hot casserole dish from the oven onto a trivet to protect the work surface. Take off the lid then quickly transfer the dough from the bowl onto the scattering of seeds and use the bench scraper to quickly roll it over so that it is covered with seeds. The dough is very sticky so don't spend time trying to shape it. Simply scoop the seed-covered mass up onto the bench scraper and drop it into the dish. Pop the lid on immediately and put it straight back into the very hot oven.

Bake for 35 minutes then remove the lid from the casserole dish while it is still in the oven and allow the crust of the bread to brown – this takes about 5–10 minutes.

Remove the casserole dish from the oven, carefully tilt it onto its side and the bread will pop out. Transfer to a cooling rack and allow to go completely cold before slicing.

TIP: Use 200g (7oz) white flour and 100g (3½oz) rye, spelt or wholemeal. as an alternative to all-white flour.

CHILD'S PLAY BISCUITS

Seems like every day is busy, time is tight, so can there ever be a circumstance when everything in life stops for long enough to make biscuits? There is an overwhelming choice in the supermarket, covering every flavour, shape, variety – oh my goodness. When the pandemic hit, people took to baking; there is something about home baking and its warming, comforting and nostalgic aromas that make it a joy to do and to taste.

Biscuits are a great quick recipe, whether you bake often or not so often, whether you are new to baking or not. In fact, for anyone wanting to begin a baking journey, biscuits are always a good foolproof place to start. I always introduce biscuits when teaching impatient children to bake, partly because they can be eaten almost immediately even though they will keep up to a week in a tin.

Biscuits are simple and quick to make, with no equipment or sharp knives required and all mixed by hand, as I think a machine overworks the dough. With a few variations on flavour (see page 150), this is a great basic recipe to return to and ring the changes.

MAKES 15–16 COOKIES

You will need

1 medium–large mixing bowl and a small bowl

baking sheet – lightly greased or lined with reusable baking parchment (see page 16)

knife, fork, teaspoon (and scissors if making the Fruit and Nut cookies)

150g (5oz) plain flour

¼ tsp baking powder

pinch of salt

90g (3oz) butter at room temperature, cubed, or coconut oil

90g (3oz) caster sugar, plus extra to dust

1 egg yolk

½ tsp vanilla extract

Preheat the oven to 180°C/350°F/gas 4 and prepare the baking sheet.

To a roomy mixing bowl, add the flour, baking powder and salt and give it a stir. Add the butter or coconut oil and rub in with the fingers until the mixture resembles breadcrumbs. Stir through the sugar (and any flavourings), then make a well in the centre and drop in the egg yolk (or add the non-dairy milk if making the vegan biscuits). Freeze the egg white to use in other recipes later (see tip on page 37).

Use a knife to mix the egg yolk (or non-dairy milk) into the mix, adding the vanilla too. Once fairly well distributed, use your hand to mould the mix into a ball of dough. It may seem really dry to begin with but keep going and the dough will come together.

Take the lined baking sheet and begin to break or cut off pieces of the dough – about 30g (1oz) each and roll into a ball between the palms. For uniformity, presentation and so that each biscuit has an even bake, each piece of dough should be weighed. This isn't as onerous as it sounds – just break off a bit and pop it on the scale before rolling. You'll soon get the feel of what the right amount is and it is so satisfying when you get it right first time. Space out the dough balls onto the baking sheet and use the back of a teaspoon to flatten them slightly. Bake for 8–10 minutes until just starting to colour, though they will still feel quite soft to the touch.

Sprinkle over a light dusting of caster sugar while hot then allow to cool and firm up. These biscuits will keep up to one week in an airtight tin or plastic box.

Chocolate Chip

Add 100g (3½oz) dark, milk or white chocolate chips to the mix when you add the sugar and stir through before adding the egg.

Vegan Chocolate Chip Cookies

Replace the butter with coconut oil, the egg yolk with 3 tbsp non-dairy milk and use 100g (3½oz) vegan dark, milk or white chocolate chips.

Cranberry and Orange Cookies

Add 80g (3oz) dried cranberries and the finely grated zest of an orange when you add the sugar and stir through before adding the egg.

Fruit and Nut Cookies

Replace the vanilla with 1 tsp almond extract, adding 50g (2oz) chopped nuts (almonds, hazelnuts, peanuts) and 50g (2oz) dried apricots (cut into small pieces with scissors) when you add the sugar.

MINI GINGERBREAD HOUSES
NEEDING ONLY ONE CUTTER

While on the subject of biscuits I decided to include these little beauties. Again, I wasn't sure which chapter they best fit, as although clearly baking, they are a bit crafty, make excellent gift ideas, amazing Christmas place settings and when filled with sweets they are treasured and adored by children.

I see so many kits on the market for making a gingerbread house, yet if you have a square cutter of any size they can easily be made at home for a fraction of the price. I like to make mini houses using just a 5cm (2 inch) square cutter and before fitting the roof, fill the house with Smarties. Children absolutely adore making and being gifted these treats and one year I used them as table decorations – we had a village in the centre of the table and each roof had a child's name piped over.

MAKES 5–6 HOUSES

You will need

large mixing bowl
wooden spoon or spatula
2 sheets of food-grade plastic (reuse cereal packet liners, see page 37)
rolling pin
5cm (2 inch) square cutter
2 baking sheets lined with baking parchment
piping bag with nozzle

icing sugar shaker
hand-held electric whisk
small bowl

FOR THE GINGERBREAD
75g (3oz) dark soft brown sugar
1 tbsp golden syrup
90g (3oz) butter
225g (8oz) plain flour
¼ tsp salt
½ tsp bicarbonate of soda
1 tsp ground ginger
1 tsp ground cinnamon
½ tsp ground cardamom (optional)
finely grated zest of 1 orange

FOR DECORATION
Royal icing – 1 egg white and 275g (9½oz) icing sugar
brown food colouring (optional)
mini sweets, for filling

In a roomy saucepan place the sugar, syrup and butter and melt over a low heat, stirring regularly. In the mixing bowl sift together the flour, salt, bicarbonate of soda and spices, then stir in the orange zest. Make a well in the centre, and when the butter has melted and the sugar dissolved, pour the liquid into the bowl of dry ingredients.

Using the wooden spoon or spatula stir well, and when cool enough to handle knead the dough into a ball. The dough is very dry and may seem crumbly, but this is important because you don't want the gingerbread to spread during baking.

Take two large pieces of plastic (I reuse the same pieces over and over again – cereal packet liners are perfect for this) and roll the dough between them. This ensures no extra flour is used and the dough doesn't stick to the worktop. Roll as thinly as you can – you want delicate little houses!

Cut out as many squares as you can, then remove the rough edges – to be re-rolled. Chill the squares for 15–20 minutes, then they will be easier to handle.

Preheat the oven to 200°C/400°F/gas 6 and take a baking sheet lined with non-stick baking parchment. You need 6 squares per house. Take the first square and roll lightly to make it slightly bigger than the rest (this will be the base). Place onto the baking sheet. Take the second square and cut it from corner to corner into two triangles (these will be the gable ends of the house), take the third and fourth squares and cut these in half horizontally (these will be the walls). The final two squares will form the roof.

Bake for 5 minutes then remove from the oven and allow to cool on the baking sheet, as the shapes are very fragile when soft.

To make the royal icing, whisk the egg white in a small bowl with an hand-held electric whisk until frothy then add the icing sugar little by little until you have a smooth, shiny, thick icing. Lemon juice or water can be added if the icing is too thick. You may want to divide your icing and colour half of it brown so that the icing for joining together your house pieces doesn't show.

Use the smallest nozzle (a hole about the size of a pin head), and the white icing, enjoy decorating your house sections, then leave to dry and set before attempting to assemble.

Take the base piece and fix first one end piece, then the two walls, then the fourth end piece. Allow to set before mounting the gable ends. Fill with sweets, if desired, then finish off with the roof pieces. Decorate the roof then dust with an icing-sugar snowstorm!

EASY AS PIE PASTRY

If you have never made pastry or when you have it has been a nightmare – let me introduce you to the easiest, most forgiving pastry dough of all – hot water crust. It has a quarter of the fat of puff pastry and half the fat of shortcrust, will not split or stick during rolling out, freezes well and is perfect for savoury pasties and pies.

There are no rules when making this dough and if you are a complete novice to pastry making, try this first because it will not go wrong. Vegans can omit the egg yolk from this dough.

Makes enough for one 23cm (9 inch) double-crust pie or 6 pasties (see pages 157-161). Any off-cuts you don't use can be frozen.

You will need

large mixing bowl
wooden spoon
wooden fork
clean cloth
250g (9oz) strong white flour (bread flour)
1 tsp salt
1 egg yolk
150ml (5fl oz) water
75g (3oz) lard, butter or vegetable shortening
1 egg yolk mixed with 1 tsp water for egg washing (vegans can use a non-dairy milk wash)

Place the flour in a roomy bowl, add the salt, then make a well to one side and drop in the egg yolk. Cover the yolk with flour then make a well at the other side of the bowl.

Add the measured water and the fat to a small saucepan and melt over a low heat, then bring to a fast boil. Immediately pour the melted fat over the flour, aiming for the second well in the flour.

I use a wooden fork to then stir everything together to a scraggy dough, then once cool enough to handle, knead briefly to a fairly smooth dough. Pop back into the bowl, cover with a cloth and leave to cool completely, then transfer to the fridge to chill and firm up for at least an hour.

Once cold this dough can be kneaded until smooth and pliable. It is less likely to stick to the work surface than other dough, will not become overworked and behaves itself and doesn't easily split or tear. It can be rolled out very thinly (the thinner the better) and makes the perfect pasties – see opposite.

CHESTNUT MUSHROOM PASTIES WITH GRAVY

Vegetarian food from scratch doesn't come any better than this. Hearty, tasty and one you will want to make again and again. The pasties and gravy freeze well (the pasties unbaked) and make excellent use of odds and ends of veg. I am often asked about gravy and in particular a vegetarian gravy. Rather than reach for the pack of instant granules – have a go at this recipe. You can freeze any surplus so that you always have it to hand. Baked from frozen, these pasties are a great quick option when you are pushed for time.

MAKES 6

You will need

18cm (7 inch) plate
sharp knife

FOR THE PASTRY
1 quantity of Easy as Pie Pastry (page 155)
1 egg, beaten with 1 tbsp water

FOR THE FILLING
1 litre (34fl oz) water with a pinch of salt
250g (9oz) chestnut mushrooms
5g dried porcini mushrooms (optional)
1 onion, finely chopped, plus 1 spring onion
1 clove of garlic, chopped

1 celery stick, cut into small dice

1 medium carrot, grated

all the trimmings from any veg prep (onion skins, carrot top and
    skin, garlic skin, pea pods, ends of celery) plus a bay leaf
    (1 dried or two fresh)

2 tbsp vegetable oil

1 tsp dried mixed herbs or 2 tsp chopped fresh herbs (sage,
    thyme, rosemary, chives, parsley)

180g (6oz) cooked whole chestnuts (I used Merchant Gourmet)

1 tsp cornflour

1 tsp grated nutmeg

1 tbsp brown sauce or barbecue sauce

80ml (3fl oz) stock (from gravy stock below)

2 tbsp cream (single, double, non-dairy or crème fraiche)

40g (1½oz) grated cheese (or non-dairy version)

salt and pepper

FOR THE GRAVY

Makes 500ml (16fl oz)

1 tbsp oil and 20g (¾oz) butter

1 onion, finely chopped

1 tbsp flour and 1 tbsp cornflour

1 heaped tsp dark brown sugar

1 vegetable stock cube (or make your own, page 36)

1 tsp dried mixed herbs and a sprinkle of dried garlic granules if
    you have them (or 1 clove of garlic, chopped)

salt and pepper, to taste

To make the filling, in a roomy saucepan bring the water with
salt to the boil then plunge the chestnut mushrooms into the
water and blanch for 2 minutes. Remove with a slotted spoon

and place in a colander to dry. Blanching the mushrooms in this way helps them to retain their flavour when fried while adding a base colour to the stock, which will be used for the gravy.

Take the pan off the heat and drop in the dried porcini mushrooms, if using, and leave for 10 minutes. Remove from the water with a slotted spoon and add to the mushrooms in the colander. Don't throw away the cooking water!

Prep the vegetables for the filling and the onion that will be used for the gravy. Pop all the peelings into the pan of mushroom liquid, bring back to the boil and allow to simmer uncovered for 10–15 minutes until reduced in volume by about half. Take from the heat and set aside – leave the veggies in the water, as they will be strained out later.

Use a large frying pan or saucepan and heat the oil. Add the finely chopped onion and cook well, until a medium golden brown then add the spring onion, garlic, celery, carrot and herbs and fry for 5 minutes until just beginning to soften.

While the onion is frying, finely chop the mushrooms, porcini and cooked chestnuts then add to the pan and stir well, increasing the heat so that the mushrooms fry dark and glossy. Fry for 5 minutes or so then reduce the heat to the lowest setting. You may see caramelization on the base of your pan which is great (flavour!) that will deglaze once the stock is added.

Add salt and pepper along with the cornflour, nutmeg and brown sauce, stir well then take just 80ml (3fl oz) liquid stock from the pan containing the peelings and stir this into the vegetables. The base of the pan will clean (deglaze) and the caramelized bits will be incorporated into your gorgeous filling. Taste and adjust the seasoning if necessary, stir through the cream then transfer to a cold bowl and set aside. Once cold stir in the grated cheese and chill until ready to use.

To make the gravy, add the oil and butter to the same pan that was used to make the filling and heat gently, then fry the finely chopped onion until well coloured (colour means flavour). Strain the pan of mushroom stock into a large jug and put the veggie trimmings onto the compost heap. Add to the fried onion in the pan, the flour, cornflour, sugar, stock cube, dried herbs, dried garlic, salt and pepper and stir well before adding the stock, little by little. Stir first to a really thick paste, then add more liquid. Increase the heat, bring to the boil and add sufficient stock until you achieve a smooth dark thick gravy. Taste and adjust the seasoning and if you prefer a smooth gravy, blitz with a hand blender.

To assemble the pasties, once chilled, the dough is very easy to work with. Divide into six pieces then roll out each thinly to a circle large enough to cut out a 18cm (7 inch) circle. I use a tea plate as a template.

Fill each circle of pastry using 3 large tablespoons of the cold filling. Dampen the edges of the pastry with water then join together at the top and down the sides, crimping to seal completely.

Place the formed pasties onto a piece of paper or baking parchment then brush with egg wash before chilling or freezing.

Preheat the oven to 200°C/400°F/gas 6 and bake from chilled for 30 minutes and from frozen for 40 minutes and until a very dark, glossy, golden brown. Serve hot with gravy poured over.

YORKSHIRE PUDDINGS

I am asked over and over again how to make a good Yorkshire pudding. A good pudding is light, very well risen, with a crisp yet soft texture. A pudding should never be hard, rubbery or doughy. It is the simplest of batters but I am amazed at the different outcomes that are seen – and some not so good even in the best establishments. They are straightforward and inexpensive to make and I am always saddened when I see plastic-packaged, factory produced, perfectly formed alternatives on the supermarket shelves. No two Yorkshires should ever look exactly the same!

A traditional Yorkshire pudding is about 7.5cm (3 inches) wide and about 5cm (2 inches) tall, and when I was a child my grandmother used to serve them on their own with gravy before the Sunday main course of roast beef. The plan was always that the Yorkshires would be so filling, there was not much room left for the very expensive beef. Any leftovers would be eaten with golden syrup, jam or lemon curd at teatime.

Nowadays we tend to serve the Yorkshire pudding, reduced in size, along with the main course. A 12-hole muffin tin is perfect and this recipe will give you 12 beautifully risen, light, golden puddings.

MAKES 12 PUDDINGS

You will need

a large mixing bowl
1 litre (34fl oz) jug and plate to cover
12-hole muffin tin

140g (5oz) plain flour

1 tsp each salt and ground white pepper

4 large eggs

140ml (5fl oz) whole milk

60ml (2fl oz) cold water (then another 20ml/¾fl oz)

20g (¾oz) beef dripping (or vegetarian alternative) shared
between the 12 cups

My 12-hole Yorkshire pudding tin (muffin tin) is used exclusively for these puds. It is blackened, well-seasoned and other than a quick wipe with a hot cloth after use doesn't get washed. The puddings never stick and they rise beautifully.

A smooth batter is essential, as a lumpy one will produce under-risen puddings. For a really smooth batter I always mix by hand using a fork.

In a large mixing bowl put the flour, salt and pepper. Make a well in the centre and drop in one of the eggs. Using a fork, mix the egg with a little of the flour, still maintaining the well in the centre. Add the remaining eggs one by one and continue to mix to a very thick mixture, bringing the flour into the egg well little by little. The batter will start to look scraggy and uneven and very thick. Keep beating this very thick mass with the fork, don't be tempted to add liquid to make the job easier. Eventually you will achieve a really thick mix – much thicker than a cake batter – but it will be smooth and without lumps.

Once you have beaten the mixture until you see that every lump of flour has been absorbed and you have a smooth yet thick dough, you can begin to add your liquids. Start by adding just a tablespoon of the milk, beat this in until it has been incorporated, then continue adding just a little at a time. Once all the milk has been incorporated, add the 60ml (2fl oz) water.

Mixing is now much easier and the batter will become the consistency of thick pouring cream and there will be no lumps.

At this stage I transfer the batter into a large jug (a jug is much easier to use when filling your tin) and place it into the fridge, covered with a plate. If you really want to get ahead, the batter can be made the day before it is needed.

When ready to make the puddings, take the Yorkshire pudding tin and place a thumbnail-sized piece of fat into each hole. Pop the tin into the cold oven then turn it on and allow to come to a temperature of 200°C/400°F/gas 6. If your oven is already switched on, allow the tin to heat for 6–8 minutes.

Take the jug of batter from the fridge and if it has been standing a long time you will find it looks unappealing and has separated a little. Perfect – you'll have the best Yorkshires! Take the other 20ml (¾fl oz) of water, add it to the jug and give the whole lot a really good beating with a fork. The batter will return to its former glory. Even if the batter hasn't had time to stand a long time and/or hasn't separated, still add the extra water because it will have thickened.

When the oven has come to temperature, or after 6–8 minutes, take the tin from the oven, the fat will be smoking and the tin will be very hot, so be careful. Pour the batter into each cup, filling to about two-thirds to three-quarters full, then pop straight back into the oven. Bake for 25 minutes in total. After 15 minutes your puddings will be well risen and brown and you may feel they are ready, but if you take them out this early they will sink. Turn the oven down to 180°C/350°F/gas 4 for the remainder of the baking time and refrain from opening the oven door. A hot oven is essential for Yorkshire puddings.

Serve immediately. You can freeze any leftovers but they are not as delicious as those made and served straight from the oven.

SOFT BUTTER SUPER TIME SAVER

How many times have you decided to bake only to find your recipe calls for 'room-temperature' butter but yours is rock hard in the fridge? This is going to slow down your baking by up to an hour! You can have room-temperature butter in minutes.

Take a small microwave-proof bowl and rinse it under the tap, then pour the water away. Place in the microwave on 'High' for 4 minutes. While the bowl is heating, weigh the amount of butter you need for your recipe then cut into 2.5-cm (1-inch) dice. Place the butter on a small plate or leave it on the butter paper. Take the hot bowl from the microwave using oven gloves then invert over the cubed butter. Leave for 4 minutes, remove the bowl and your butter is soft, non-oily and ready to be creamed.

GREEN TOMATO CAKES

If you grow your own tomatoes, even on a small patio or garden (see Time to Grow, page 279), there will be the inevitable stubborn under-ripe 'greenies' left over at the close of the season. When I was a child I remember being given the job of wrapping each green tomato in its own square of newspaper so that they would ripen in their own time, the semi-ripe ones were stood side by side on a sunny windowsill, some would go into chutney but never into cake. If you slice a green tomato and taste it, it really is quite yummy, almost apple-like, being firm and not too juicy and with a tart sweetness, so I decided to give it a go. This recipe can be easily adjusted to make it gluten-free.

MAKES 12 MUFFINS OR 12 SLICES

You will need

food processor
colander
2 plates – 1 large dinner plate and 1 tea plate
medium-sized mixing bowl
hand-held electric whisk
ice-cream scoop
12-hole deep muffin tin lined with paper cases or a 20cm
    (8 inch) square cake (not loose-bottomed) tin brushed with
    lining paste (page 131) or 2 x 450g (1lb) or 1 x 900g (2lb) loaf
    tin brushed with lining paste

FOR THE CAKE

250g (9oz) green tomatoes

1 tsp salt

150g (5oz) soft brown sugar (if you are out of brown sugar turn
to page 21 and make your own)

150ml (5fl oz) vegetable, sunflower or rapeseed oil

3 eggs

150g (5oz) self-raising flour (see home-blended on page 17)
(or gluten-free flour)

50g (2oz) ground almonds (or ground rice for those with nut
allergies)

1 tsp ground cinnamon

1 tsp grated nutmeg

2–3 tbsp sugar nibs for decoration if not using a frosting
(optional)

FOR THE FROSTING

60g (2oz) room-temperature butter

60g (2oz) icing sugar

100g (3½oz) full-fat cream cheese

1 tsp vanilla extract

2 tbsp toasted flaked almonds for decoration

Start by cutting the tomatoes into halves, or quarters if larger
than the size of an egg, then pop them into a food processor
with the blade fitted and blitz for a few seconds until the fruits
are roughly chopped but not puréed. Transfer to a colander
standing on a plate, sprinkle over the salt and lay over a plate
with a weight and leave for at least an hour (or even overnight)
to make sure any excess juice is extracted.

Preheat the oven to 180°C/350°F/gas 4.

In a roomy mixing bowl whisk together the sugar and the oil and make sure there are no lumps in the brown sugar before you start. Once well mixed whisk in the eggs and continue to whisk until the mixture is smooth – about 2 minutes.

Fold in all of the dry ingredients – the flour, almonds (or ground rice), cinnamon and nutmeg – and once all is well combined, add the drained tomatoes.

This is a thin batter so I find it easier to use an ice-cream scoop to transfer to the 12 paper cupcake cases. If making the cake or baking in loaf tins, pour straight into the prepared tins. Bake the cake for 35–40 minutes and the cupcakes for 25–30 minutes.

I add sugar nibs to cakes that I am not going to ice, and these should be scattered over when the cakes have been in the oven for around 10 minutes so that the sugar doesn't sink. Taking care not to burn yourself – just sprinkle them over the cakes without taking them out of the oven.

Once baked, remove from the oven and place on a cooling rack. If you want to apply a cream cheese frosting wait until the cakes are completely cooled.

Whisk together the butter and sugar until pale and fluffy then add the cream cheese, little by little and finally the vanilla. Spread over the cake and sprinkle over flaked almonds. Cut into 12 slices.

This cake with the frosting will last 2–3 days in a tin in a cool place. Without the frosting it will keep for about a week in a tin and can be frozen. The frosted cake is not suitable for freezing.

PERFECT SHORTCRUST PASTRY

Many people tell me they can't make pastry. I am told so often that results are too 'hit and miss', it gets too messy, there isn't the time and in our fast and furious life it is far easier to buy a block from the supermarket.

I totally get it, and buying a block is fine but before you do and before you read the number of ingredients on the back of the packet (up to 12 in some cases) and become a consumer of another single-use piece of plastic, I urge you to try my two-minute method, which costs less, contains just four ingredients and freezes well. No plastic, preservatives or palm oil, and it tastes much better.

Even if you don't do this every time, try it and once you are familiar with the ingredients and method I think you will begin to turn your back on the mass-produced version. I always make double the amount below – one now and one for the freezer. I may even line a tart tin with the pastry dough and freeze it, then my next tart is already halfway done.

I call this my 'shortcut' pastry and I actually surprised myself when I timed the making, which included weighing out the ingredients. Everything goes into the bowl together, whizz and you're done! No guess work and it's failsafe.

You will need

food processor
2 sheets of food-grade plastic (reuse cereal packet liners, see
    page 37)

rolling pin

8oz (225g) plain flour

pinch of salt

4oz (115g) chilled butter, cut into dice (or vegetable shortening cut into dice and frozen for 30 minutes)

4 tbsp cold water

I place the bowl of the food processor with the blade attached onto my weighing scales set to pounds and ounces (not grams). You will see that all other recipes in this book are stated in metric first, but for shortcrust pastry **alone** I use imperial weights – and this is why.

Pastry texture is affected through adding too much water or too little water. Too much water and the dough is sticky, more flour has to be added and the resulting pastry is hard and tough. Not enough water and the dough is crumbly, doesn't come together well, is very difficult to handle and won't hold together when baked.

My little recipe calculated in 'pounds and ounces' gives exactly the amount of water to add and you will not go wrong. Try to remember for a basic dough you need half-fat to flour and then for every ounce of fat you need 1 tablespoon of liquid. Retain those basic rules and you will have a perfect pastry every time.

Measure the flour first then add a pinch of salt. Reset the scales to zero then weigh in the chilled cubed butter and drizzle over the cold water.

Pop the bowl onto the machine, securing the blade, then on with the lid and blitz for 20–30 seconds until the ingredients are transformed from a crumb to a lump of dough. And that is it. Two minutes all in!

Remove the dough from the machine, briefly knead to a smooth ball then wrap in greaseproof paper or a beeswax wrap (see page 211) and chill for half an hour or pop into the freezer for later.

Now you have the perfect ball of dough – we don't want to alter the texture by adding flour to roll out. I have found that rolling between two sheets of food-grade plastic the perfect solution: cereal packet liners! (See page 37.) If you don't have cereal packet liners, two large freezer bags – each cut down one side and across the bottom – will give two large pieces of food-grade plastic, though you'll have an annoying crease down the centre. The plastics (cereal packets or freezer bags) can be washed and used over and over.

Using two sheets of plastic with the ball of dough in between start to roll from the centre outwards. The plastic can be moved around, no extra flour is required, no sticking and the rolled-out dough can be lifted up to the light to detect any thick bits and then be slid onto a baking sheet and into the fridge until you need to bake it. The fridge is your friend when working with pastry. Popping a pastry case into the fridge while preparing a filling is always a good idea. I always chill a prepared pie or tart before transferring to the oven.

TRADITIONAL LEMON MERINGUE PIE

This next recipe is for my lemon meringue pie, and I have decided to include it because it is my favourite of all pastry bakes, however, it took me years to perfect. I had tried and tested so many recipes, some resulting in the soggiest pastry that refused to lift from the tin, others with runny lemon fillings that could only be eaten with a large soup spoon and a meringue which, once taken out of the oven, decided to slide off the top of the pie in one large piece. After many trials and lots of errors, though, this is my perfect bake.

Lemon meringue pie made properly has a perfect balance of everything you need from a dessert. Sweet yet crispy and tart. A slice of my lemon meringue pie will have a thin, light crust, a firm tart-lemon custard and topped with a pillow of meringue that has a thin crispy shell. Perfect.

I don't know anyone who doesn't drool when you tell them that it is on the menu, and thankfully it is one of those fabulous recipes that can be made ahead of time.

You will need

food processor
2 sheets of food-grade plastic (reuse cereal packet liners, see page 37)
rolling pin
a loose-bottomed flan tin or deep pie plate 23cm (9in) in diameter, lightly greased or brushed with lining paste
baking beans

serrated knife

spatula or palette knife

large mixing bowl

hand-held electric whisk

reusable piping bag and plain 1cm (½ inch) nozzle (optional)

FOR THE PASTRY

175g (6oz) plain flour and a pinch of salt

75g (3oz) chilled butter, diced

3 tbsp cold water

FOR THE FILLING

finely grated zest and juice of 2 lemons

250ml (8fl oz) cold water

3½ tbsp cornflour

40g (1½oz) butter, at room temperature

2 egg yolks

50g (2oz) caster sugar

FOR THE TOPPING

2 egg whites

100g (3½oz) icing sugar, sifted

1 tsp cream of tartar or 1 tsp cornflour

While the pastry is being rolled out, preheat the oven to 200°C/400°F/gas 6. Begin by making the pastry using the two-minute method (see page 169). Wrap in greaseproof paper or beeswax wrap (see page 211) and chill in the fridge for half an hour.

Roll out the pastry thinly (to about the thickness of a £1 coin) and line the tin, allowing surplus pastry to hang over the edges.

Prick the base of the pastry shell with a fork, then line it with a piece of greaseproof paper and weigh it down with baking beans. Blind-bake for 12 minutes until the pastry is firm. Remove the paper and baking beans then pop the shell back into the oven for a further 3–4 minutes to ensure the base is fully dried out and golden brown. The blind-baked shell should feel dry when touched with the finger. If there are any grey or dense-looking areas, pop it back into the oven for a further 2–3 minutes.

Take from the oven and immediately turn the temperature down to 150°C/300°F/gas 2, then trim the rough pastry edge while still warm – I use a small serrated knife and small sawing actions.

During the time the pastry case is baking, make the lemon filling. In a small saucepan over a low heat, place all the filling ingredients and stir continually until the butter and sugar dissolve and the mixture starts to thicken, about 4–5 minutes.

Transfer the thick lemon filling into the cooked pastry case and smooth over with the back of a spoon or palette knife. Allow to stand a few minutes to form a skin while you mix the meringue.

In a spotlessly clean, grease-free bowl, whisk the egg whites until they are fairly thick and stand in peaks when the whisk is removed. Sift the icing sugar and cream of tartar (or cornflour) together, then add this one large spoonful at a time, whisking well between each addition. The final meringue will be very thick, glossy and luscious.

Pipe or spoon the meringue onto the lemon filling, ensuring it covers all of the lemon cream (see tip opposite) then bake in the low-temperature oven for 40 minutes until the meringue has a slightly tinged, crisp crust. To prevent the meringue from cracking, leave to cool in the oven with the oven door ajar.

The finished lemon meringue pie can be served warm or cold.

TIPS: When piling or piping the meringue onto the pie, start at the outside and work inwards, making sure you seal all the way around the edge. Finish in the middle. That way you will not get any of the lemon leaking out of the pie.

I find sifted icing sugar with cream of tartar or cornflour whisks to a very thick, smooth, dense meringue, which dries out perfectly in the oven giving a crispy top but a light, mousse-like meringue layer underneath.

If you want to get ahead, the pastry case can be baked blind and stored in an airtight tin once cold for 2–3 days. On the day of serving, mix the lemon filling, pour into the case and leave to cool completely. Then pop the whisked-up meringue over and bake in a low oven as above when you are ready.

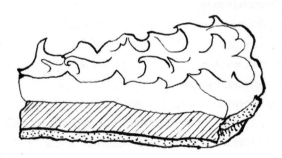

PASTRY OFFCUTS

I hear my grandmother's voice ringing in my ears 'Never throw away pastry dough'. If you are left with the smallest amount, pop it into a freezer bag or box and the next time you make pastry, marry the two lots of trimmings together to make something yummy. The quickest recipe I know for using up shortcrust pastry offcuts is my grandmother's Jam Pasty.

Jam Pasty

You will need

shortcrust pastry offcuts – any more than 100g (3½oz) is perfect
2 sheets of food-grade plastic (reuse cereal-packet liners, see page 37)
rolling pin
pizza cutter or knife
baking sheet lined with greaseproof paper
fruit jam
egg or milk, to wash
caster sugar, to sprinkle

Preheat the oven to 200°C/400°F/gas 6. Roll out the pastry offcuts as thinly as possible then square off using a pizza cutter or knife. Transfer the piece of dough to a greased baking sheet or one lined with a piece of reusable baking parchment.

Dampen the outside 1cm (½ inch) edge of the pastry with

water then spread fruit jam over one half of the dough. The jam needs to be an even coat, not too thick because it will bubble over – about the thickness you would spread on bread or scones. Fold over the other side, covering the jam. Gently press on the dampened edge to secure and flute using the back of a knife to seal the pasty. Make a series of air holes with the point of a knife, brush with beaten egg or just milk and bake in the oven for about 20 minutes until golden brown.

Take from the oven and while hot sprinkle over a dusting of caster sugar. Once cool, cut into even-sized pieces. I like to cut into squares and eat like a posh biscuit. Believe it or not this is delicious!

The Quickest Fruit Tart

Around 200g (7oz) puff pastry offcuts will produce an elegant yet super simple, open fruit tart. Served warm with a blob of cream or ice cream for a family dessert that will use up gluts of fruit too.

You will need

rolling pin
2 baking sheets lined with reusable baking parchment
23cm (9in) loose bottom from a cake tin to use as a template
pizza cutter or vegetable knife
small bowl or saucer
pastry brush
plain flour, for dusting
180–200g (6–7oz) puff pastry offcuts
2 tbsp ground almonds

1 tbsp icing sugar, plus extra for dusting

1 tbsp lemon juice

2–3 small dessert apples (or use firm pears, nectarines, plums, apricots)

2 tbsp apricot jam

1 tsp water

Preheat the oven to 200°C/400°F/gas 6 with one baking sheet inside.

||||||||||||||||||||||||||||||||||||||||||||||||||||||||||||||||||||||||||||||||||||||||||||||||||||||||||||||||||||||||||||||

TIP: Only have one flat baking sheet but this recipe calls for two? Upturn a roasting tin and use the flat base uppermost in the oven.

||||||||||||||||||||||||||||||||||||||||||||||||||||||||||||||||||||||||||||||||||||||||||||||||||||||||||||||||||||||||||||||

Lightly flour a work surface then roll out the dough as thinly as possible to a size exceeding 23cm (9in) in diameter. Lay the circle of dough over the rolling pin and transfer to the sheet of reusable baking parchment set on a baking sheet. Use a pizza cutter or vegetable knife to cut out a circle using a 23cm (9in) loose bottom or cake tin as a template.

Sprinkle over the ground almonds followed by the icing sugar, maintaining a 1cm (½ inch) clear border around the edge of the dough.

Measure the lemon juice into a small bowl then cut the apples into quarters, remove the core but not the skin. Slice the apples very thinly then dip into lemon juice before arranging them around the edge of the tart base, overlapping as you go. The lemon juice will prevent the apple slices turning brown. Continue arranging the apple slices, finishing at the centre.

Use the blunt edge of the vegetable knife to gently knock up the sides of the dough, this will encourage the layers to rise up higher than the fruit layer during baking.

Remove the preheated baking sheet from the hot oven and carefully slide the tart onto it. This will immediately seal the dough, ensuring the base bakes thoroughly and there's no soggy bottom. Pop it back into the oven and bake for 20–25 minutes until the apples are beginning to tinge with colour at the edges and the pastry dough is brown.

While the tart is baking, spoon the apricot jam into a saucepan with the water and heat gently until the jam is thin and runny. Take the tart from the oven and while still hot use the pastry brush to apply the warm apricot glaze over each apple slice.

Once cool enough to handle, transfer to a presentation plate, dust with icing sugar and serve with ice cream or cream. I find a pizza cutter ideal for cutting into neat slices.

THE BEST CHOCOLATE BUTTERCREAM

Leftover egg whites will freeze perfectly (see page 37), then I have them to hand when I want to make a perfect buttercream rather than mixing a batch of sickly sweet standard filling. This is a firm favourite. I urge you to give it a go. It is not difficult, no special kit or thermometers are required, and once you have mastered it, there is no going back.

Chocolate Swiss Meringue Buttercream

MAKES ENOUGH TO FILL A 20 OR 23CM (8 OR 9 INCH)
CHOCOLATE CAKE

You will need

hand-held electric whisk
60g (2oz) dark chocolate chips
70g (3oz) light soft brown sugar
1 egg white
125g (4½oz) room-temperature butter
1 tbsp cocoa powder mixed to a thin paste with 3–4 tbsp milk
   and ½ tsp vanilla extract

Start by melting the chocolate as this needs to be cool before using. Pop the chips into a non-metallic bowl and microwave in two 20-second bursts, which is sufficient to cause the chocolate to melt. Stir then set aside.

Place the sugar in a roomy mixing bowl making sure there are no lumps in it, then add the egg white. Give everything a good stir. Place the bowl over a pan of barely simmering water, with the bottom of the bowl not touching the water, and stir with a spatula until the sugar is dissolved and the mixture is pale in colour.

Once there is no gritty feel to the mixture (test by rubbing a little of it between a thumb and forefinger and it should feel smooth), take the electric whisk and mix, still over the heat, until the mixture thickens, turns pale in colour and doubles in size.

Take the bowl off the pan of water and transfer onto a folded cloth on your work surface to prevent it slipping or sliding. Continue to mix until the meringue, while still being thick, pale and gorgeous will be cool. This can take about 5 minutes. Set aside.

In the second bowl, whisk the soft butter until creamy then add the cooled meringue, one spoonful at a time, whisking well between each addition. Finally add the melted chocolate and cocoa powder paste. I always add flavours to buttercream last of all.

This cream is silky, not too sweet and will keep, covered, for up to one week in the fridge.

Vanilla

Use white sugar in place of brown
1–2 tsp vanilla extract, omitting the chocolate and cocoa

Lemon

Use white sugar in place of brown
Whisk in a half quantity of lemon curd (see page 134), omitting
the chocolate and cocoa

Coffee

Use 2 tbsp instant coffee and ½ tsp vanilla extract dissolved in
2–3 tbsp warm water, omitting the chocolate and cocoa

TIME TO CELEBRATE THE SPUD!

wanted to spend some time on the gorgeous potato but I wasn't sure whether to include this in the Growing chapter or Cooking chapter so I decided, as the potato tends to be overlooked somewhat, I would instead devote a chapter to this gorgeous food.

When I thought about the potato I realized I have never heard anyone say they don't like them. Some say they're not keen on mash or have decided they're cutting down on the calories and laying off chips or crisps for a while, but most of us just love them in their various preparations. Potatoes are rich in vitamins, minerals and antioxidants, which makes them very healthy – they are cheap, easy to grow, versatile, zero waste and a staple food in my home.

I wanted to spend a little time explaining how I grow potatoes every year, offer a few recipes that are a bit different, celebrate the fact that we can eat every morsel of the potato and rejoice in the fact that it can be enjoyed by everyone – whether vegan, vegetarian, dairy- or gluten-free.

The potato was originally cultivated in the South American Andes, where they were grown for many thousands of years before being brought to Europe in the mid-1500s. Sir Walter Raleigh introduced potatoes to Ireland in 1589 and by 1597 they had reached London. After that very brief history lesson, I will now talk about growing them at home.

GROWING YOUR OWN

I grow a few rows of potatoes every year because until you have tasted your own freshly dug potatoes, rubbed their skins off and steamed or boiled for just a few minutes there is not a flavour or texture to match it. No shop can capture the freshness and distinct taste of home-grown new potatoes. These are a 'once a year' treat and it is this that makes them special.

Potatoes fall into three categories: First Earlies, Second Earlies and Maincrop. I grow First Earlies – planted around Easter time and ready for harvesting at the end of June in the UK. Potatoes take up quite a lot of space, so once the potatoes have vacated their growing spot I can continue to sow veggies there for later in the season. 'Earlies' can go straight into the kitchen, whereas later crops must be dried before storing in the winter.

Second Earlies are a later new potato and Maincrop are those larger, thicker-skinned potatoes that will be harvested and stored to see us all through the winter.

How to prepare potatoes for planting

I buy seed potatoes in January or February. There are many varieties to choose from, though I tend to stick to my 'old faithful'. My grandad used to grow Arran Pilot and I stick with what I consider to be the best. Some say their flavour surpasses that of Jersey Royals.

When examining a seed potato it looks like any potato but it's smaller, about the size of an egg. On closer examination it is possible to see the 'eyes' – tiny dots on the skin which will eventually sprout and bear their own family of potatoes.

As the days grow longer and the weather gets warmer these 'eyes' will sprout. Have you ever gone to your supermarket bag of potatoes in March or April to find spooky white tubes wrapped around them? These potatoes have attempted to grow shoots and are searching for light.

Seed potatoes need to be prevented from doing this. The potatoes are spaced out, given light and a cool place to 'chit' (encouraged to sprout) for about six weeks. There is a bottom and top to a seed potato and once the eyes begin to sprout you will see that the base of the potato has no sprouting whereas the top of the potato has. Try to ensure the sprouting potato is facing upwards in its box.

TIP: Save egg boxes or trays, as these are perfect for potato chitting. The cardboard moulds keep the potatoes upright, the soft material doesn't damage the shoots and the open design offers them plenty of light.

When I get my seed potatoes home I take them straight from the pack and lay the small egg-sized potatoes into a large egg tray. The potatoes need to be in a cool but light, frost-free place. My pantry is perfect for this. I stand the egg boxes on the wide windowsill.

Chitting results in, over a period of six weeks, the eyes growing a dark, purple sprout with just the hint of a dark green leaf at the end. Once these shoots have grown to about 1–2cm (½–¾ inch) they are ready for planting.

Potting and Planting

I grow potatoes in a 'v'-shaped trench dug around 20cm (8 inches) deep. Potatoes can also be planted in pots, in fact any container with a depth of about 60cm (2 feet). Potatoes are not too fussy and will grow in any soil, though the best results will be achieved by adding good compost the previous autumn, which I rake over the bed. I don't 'double-dig' as used to be the accepted way (digging the hole to the depth of two spades), I simply dig over in October or November to remove weeds and break up the soil, then I sprinkle over a dressing of well-rotted compost and leave the worms, rain and frost to do their work in aerating the soil.

I plant my potatoes out into the vegetable beds in late March at around Easter time. The soil needs to be warming up, so if there is snow on the ground or the soil is cold, wet, hard or frosty, leave it a week or two. For those with less space, potatoes are not fussy and can be grown in large pots or any large container as long as it has drainage holes.

After marking the row with string I have a very old 'draw hoe', which is very handy for creating the trench. The soil piles high either side of the little trench, then I pop my chitted spuds 30cm (1 foot) apart in it, with the shoots facing up.

I don't want to disturb any of those fresh shoots, so I set them onto a good handful of soft compost and if the grass has been cut and there are fresh clippings (not treated with fertilizer, weedkiller or the like), I sprinkle them over each potato. This keeps them moist, protects the little shoots and will help defend them against attacks of potato fungus.

I then carefully pull the soil over to cover the potatoes using a garden rake and create a mound of earth above the row to about 30cm (1 foot) in depth. This 'earthing up' of the row will protect the growing potatoes from frost, keep them moist and will encourage heavier crops. It also keeps the potatoes well buried so that they will not turn green through exposure to light. Green potatoes are toxic and should not be eaten.

That's it for me – I am sure there are potato-growing experts who suggest doing much more but I now just wait for the green leaf shoots to appear, and keep the bed weed-free and well-watered.

I am often asked how to know when potato crops are ready. Early or 'new' potatoes are eaten immature in early summer, when they are no larger than an egg. Once I see a purple flower appear on any of the plants I will have a look by carefully moving the soil away with my hand and scraping down until I find a potato and see whether it is large enough to eat. It can be covered up again if not.

Dig up the potatoes as you need them day by day, because after lifting they soon lose flavour. A potato fork with its flat, blunt tines greatly cuts down the risk of damaging or slicing though the potatoes when digging, though if you haven't grown many, getting down on your hands and knees and uplifting with a hand trowel is even more satisfying.

Enjoy your potato crop.

I never get fed up with potatoes – fried, mashed, jackets – and I add in here my favourite potato recipes, which have been hugely popular with social media followers.

BOULANGÈRE POTATOES

This is one of my favourite potato recipes; lighter than dauphinoise and in my opinion even more tasty. The advantage of this recipe is that it can serve one, two or four, be doubled or trebled to serve a crowd, and unbaked portions can be frozen after the first cooking then finished and baked from frozen when required. This recipe can be adapted and enjoyed by vegetarians, vegans and those sticking to a gluten-free diet.

SERVES 6

You will need

an ovenproof dish or tin, oiled or brushed with lining paste (see page 131) – my tin measures 23 x 15 x 6cm (9 x 6 x 2 inches) deep

food processor or mandolin

baking sheet

1 onion, finely sliced

15g (1 tbsp) butter (or non-dairy alternative), plus extra for frying (optional)

500g (1lb 2oz) prepared weight of potatoes (peeled and sliced very thinly using a mandolin or food processor – or the thinnest you can do with a knife)

3 cloves of garlic, chopped

3 tbsp chopped sage or chives, or 1½ tbsp mixed dried herbs

1 heaped tsp plain flour (or gluten free flour)

100ml (3½fl oz) hot chicken or vegetable stock

100ml (3½fl oz) milk (or non-dairy alternative)
2 tbsp finely grated Parmesan cheese (or non-dairy alternative)
salt and pepper, to taste

Preheat the oven to 180°C/375°F/gas 4.

You can use raw onions but I have found a better flavour by frying them for 5–10 minutes with a knob of butter or a tablespoon of oil until they have softened and turned a light golden brown.

Start with an even layer of the sliced potatoes, onion, garlic, seasoning and herbs and layer the remaining potatoes evenly on top. Sprinkle over the flour then pour over the stock and milk. Dot the butter in blobs over the top.

Cover the dish in a layer of buttered or greased baking paper and bake in the oven for 50 minutes to an hour. Check to make sure the potatoes are tender, and if they still feel hard when you inside the point of a knife from top to bottom, pop them back into the oven for a further 30 minutes.

If you want to serve straight away: remove the paper from the potatoes once cooked, scatter over the Parmesan cheese and bake for a further 25 minutes until brown and crispy on the top.

If you want to prepare ahead: take the dish from the oven once the potatoes are tender, leave the paper on and allow to cool completely. When completely cold, peel away the piece of baking paper and grate over the Parmesan cheese.

When ready to serve, cut the cold block of cooked potato into even-sized square or oblong portions. Use a fish slice to transfer to a baking sheet that's lightly greased or lined with baking parchment and reheat for 15–20 minutes at 200°C/400°F/gas 6 until the potatoes are browned, bubbling and smelling absolutely delicious.

TIP: Portions can be frozen at the stage where the potatoes are cut into squares, wrap each portion in a cereal-packet liner or store in a freezerproof container. When ready to cook, simply transfer to a preheated baking sheet and bake from frozen for 30–40 minutes or until bubbling and crispy on the top.

BABY HASSELBACKS

Every bag of potatoes contains the small fiddly ones that once peeled are no bigger than the size of an egg. They can be too small for 'jackets' or chips yet are perfect for hasselbacks. As long as the potatoes are washed and dried, there is no need to peel them. Avoid them floundering unused in the bottom of the sack with this easy recipe.

You will need

a metal skewer
baking tin or sheet
pastry brush
6 potatoes, each around the size of a very large egg
50g (2oz) butter
1 tsp dried mixed herbs
1 tsp garlic granules
salt and pepper, to taste
finely chopped chives or parsley, to garnish

Preheat the oven to 200°C/400°F/gas 6. Begin by washing and drying the potatoes. I give mine a scrub then dry them on a clean tea towel.

Work on a chopping board. Taking the metal skewer, facing downwards onto the board, not upwards towards you. Stand the potato upright on the board and pierce with the skewer about one-third in from one side, all the way through until the point of the skewer hits the board. Turn the potato on its side and continue to push the skewer through so that you have an inch or two showing at the base of the potato.

Take a vegetable knife and make a series of cuts through the broadest side of the potato. The 'fins' need to be about 5mm (¼ inch) wide. Cut along the potato at equal distances, the skewer will prevent the cuts going all the way through. Pull out the skewer, place the potato on the baking sheet or tin then repeat with the rest of the potatoes.

Melt the butter in a saucepan then add the herbs and garlic. Take each potato and gently part the fins using your fingers and brush over with the flavoured melted butter. Try to brush between each fin – the finished product will look much more appealing and hold more flavour if you take a little time at this stage.

Finish with a grinding of salt and pepper then transfer to the oven and bake for 45 minutes to an hour (depending on the size of the potatoes). Test they are done by piercing with the point of a vegetable knife – there should be no resistance.

I like to scatter over finely chopped chives or parsley. These potatoes are delicious!

OVEN MASH

I adore creamy mashed potatoes! Yet when making them, how many of us have them bubbling away on the stove top or hob while the oven is on cooking the casserole or roast? We can save precious fuel and money by cooking the potatoes in the oven alongside the main meal.

You will need

an ovenproof pan or casserole dish with a well-fitting lid
4–6 (around 1kg/2¼lb peeled weight) potatoes
1 tsp salt

FOR MASHING
70g (3oz) butter
a little ground white pepper
170–200ml (6–7fl oz) whole milk

Preheat the oven: the temperature of the oven isn't too important – they can join whatever is being cooked at the same time. If the oven is on at 200°C/400°F/gas 6 the potatoes will take around 30 minutes. If the oven is on at 170°C/325°F/gas 3 the potatoes could take around 45–50 minutes.

Peel the potatoes and cut into walnut-sized pieces, then place them in the ovenproof pan or casserole dish. Sprinkle over the salt. Bring the kettle to the boil (remember a full kettle of water is not required, just boil up what you need), then pour over sufficient boiling water around the potatoes so that it comes about 2.5cm (1 inch) up the side of the pan. Immediately it's on with the lid, then transfer to the hot oven.

Take from the oven once cooked, off with the lid and check to make sure they are cooked through by inserting the point of a vegetable knife – there should be no resistance – then pour off any remaining liquid. There will be very little. Mash the potatoes as normal with butter, milk, pepper or your favourite flavourings. The measurements of butter and milk above are my go-to but mash is a very personal thing, so you may want to adjust to taste.

Apart from the obvious cost saving to cooking potatoes in this way, more nutrients are saved because the potatoes steam rather than boil – no steamy windows, no pan boiling over or boiling dry. Any root vegetable can be cooked in this way.

REFRESH MASH

Leftover cold mashed potato is not too appealing but it is great used in fish cakes and bubble and squeak. If you want to refresh your leftover mash to use as 'mash', it can be taken from the hard, unappealing cold state to its former fluffy, creamy gorgeousness in minutes. Refreshing old mash is a great standby when making a shepherd's pie or fish pie, as half of the job is then done for you. It is worth making extra mash on Sunday to use this way early on in the week.

You will need

wooden fork
leftover mash – say 300g (10½oz)
20g (¾oz) butter
20g (¾oz) milk

Place the solid lump of cold mashed potato into a microwave-proof bowl and break it up with a wooden fork. Pop into the microwave, uncovered, on High for 1–2 minutes. Give the mash a stir with the fork then add the butter and milk.

Microwave on High in one-minute bursts, taking from the microwave, giving it a good beating with the wooden fork then returning for another minute. After 3 minutes in total, or depending how much mash is being refreshed, the creamy fluffy consistency and fresh mash taste will have returned.

Sprinkle a little grated cheese over the mash if you're using it to top off your fish pie or shepherd's pie.

LUXURY FISH PIE

This fish pie is a tradition in our household on Good Friday and I double, treble and quadruple the ingredients to feed a crowd. I think individual bowls (deep ovenproof soup bowls or similar) are lovely for a special occasion and if you are feeling particularly ambitious you can pipe the mashed potato before sprinkling over a grating of Parmesan (or any) cheese.

The quantities here will make three or four individual pies or one large family pie. An unbaked fish pie made with fresh fish, not previously frozen, will freeze perfectly.

It is worth making extra mash for another meal, which can be refreshed and used to top off this pie (see page 197).

SERVES 4

You will need

3–4 ovenproof soup bowls or an ovenproof dish measuring approx. 25 x 20 x 5cm (10 x 8 x 2 inches)

FOR THE FISH FILLING

400g (14oz) mixed fresh filleted fish (salmon, haddock, cod) cut into 2cm (¾ inch) cubes

50g (2oz) prawns, cooked or uncooked

25g (1oz) butter

1 small onion or shallot, finely chopped

1 small leek, thinly sliced

20g (1oz) plain flour, plus 1 tbsp cornflour

150ml (5fl oz) whole milk

150ml (5fl oz) fish stock (made with a stock cube but make it
   double concentrate)
2 tbsp capers, chopped
2 tbsp fresh chopped parsley, tarragon, fennel or dill (or 1 tbsp
   dried)
1 tsp grated nutmeg
½ tsp each salt and pepper
zest and juice of 1 lemon

FOR THE MASH
3–4 medium potatoes, peeled and boiled
120ml (4fl oz) whole milk
40g (1½oz) butter
1 tbsp mayonnaise or salad cream
salt and pepper, to taste
OR
Use 300g–400g (10½–14oz) refreshed mash, see page 197
4 tbsp grated Parmesan cheese (or any cheese to sprinkle over)

Start by placing the fish and prawns in a roomy mixing bowl.
In a small saucepan melt the butter then add the onion and
leek and fry until softened but not browned. Add the flour
and cornflour and stir until you have a very thick paste, then
gradually add the milk, a little at a time, stirring; that way you
will avoid lumps. Then add the fish stock and place over a
medium heat, stirring all the time until you have a thick sauce.
The sauce should be the consistency of thick whipped cream.
Set aside to cool.

Transfer the sauce to the bowl of fish once cold, then add
the capers, herbs, nutmeg, salt and pepper and lemon zest and
juice. Stir well then transfer to the dish/es.

Boil 3–4 potatoes until there is no resistance when pierced with a knife, then mash until very smooth with the milk, butter and other ingredients, or use refreshed leftover mash. Pipe or spread the mash over the fish mixture.

The fish pie or pies can be chilled for up to 8 hours before cooking or can be frozen until required. Bake chilled pies for 50 minutes at 200°C/400°F/gas 6 or cook from frozen for 1 hour 10 minutes. The fish pie needs to be dark golden and bubbling. Leave for 10 minutes to rest before serving, as it is impossibly hot to eat straight from the oven.

POTATO PEEL CRISPS

These are great to nibble on rather than reaching for a plastic bag of crisps. Use root vegetable peelings, too.

Use a potato peeler or speed peeler to remove thin layers of skin from your washed and dried potatoes, then pop the peels into a bowl, drizzle over a tablespoon of oil for skins from every 2 large potatoes, plus a little salt and a good grating of pepper. I then add ½ teaspoon of garlic powder and a teaspoon of paprika.

For a change, in place of paprika use dried mixed herbs, curry powder, a few chilli flakes, crushed fennel seeds – there are lots of options.

Mix around with the hands until the skins are glossy and coated, then spread out onto a baking tray and cook for 8–10 minutes at 200°C/400°F/gas 6 until the skins become golden and crispy. Transfer to a bowl lined with a piece of crumpled greaseproof paper, scatter over a few sea salt flakes. I like to serve these with a drink before dinner is ready!

JUICY JACKETS!

One of the finest things in life is the perfect jacket potato! I like mine crispy on the outside and meltingly soft and squidgy on the inside. Overdone and the skin is wrinkled, hard and the potato inside shrunken away and dry. Underdone and the potato skin is soft, the inside hard and doesn't soak up the butter, cheese or other toppings.

The jacket potato can't be rushed, so give it the right amount of time and choose evenly sized potatoes so that they will all cook well together. Jackets are perfect to cook when the oven is on for something else – spuds are not fussy!

Smaller jacket potatoes can also accompany a main meal – see my midweek Chilli with jackets or rice on page 58.

SERVES 4

4 large baking potatoes – each weighing 160–180g (5–6oz)
2 tsp oil
1 tbsp salt flakes (or simple table salt)

Preheat the oven to 200°C/400°F/gas 6. The potatoes need to be scrubbed clean and thoroughly dried before baking. If you can remember, wash the potatoes in advance and leave them to dry. When ready to bake, allow 1 hour to 1 hour 15 minutes.

Prick each potato two to three times with a fork then rub the oil over your hands and rub all over the potato skins before giving each a sprinkle of salt. The oil and salt will ensure a crispy skin and piercing it with a fork will prevent the skin splitting.

Place the potatoes on a high shelf in the oven for 20 minutes, then I quickly turn them over and turn the temperature down slightly to 180°C/375°F/gas 4 and leave them to complete their cooking, which will take around 50 minutes.

To test whether the potatoes are done, all they need is a gentle squeeze, but be careful because they are hot. The potato should feel soft.

Take from the oven, pop onto serving plates and I make a cross in the top with a sharp knife and squeeze the potato from the sides, pushing the flesh upwards. Top off with a filling of choice. Here are my favourites:

Knob of butter, a little flaked tuna mixed with sweetcorn and snipped chives

Grated cheese, chopped cooked bacon and spring onions

Chilli – see page 58, with a dressing of fresh red chilli and coriander leaves

Fried mushrooms, grated nutmeg and cream with a sprinkling of fresh thyme

TIP: A snip of fresh home-grown herbs takes an ordinary easy meal to the next level and herbs are easy to grow yourself at home.

POTATO SALAD

I have included this simple recipe, which is an ideal solution if there are leftover new potatoes or indeed if you want a tasty accompaniment to barbecue foods and salads in the summer or cold cuts in the winter.

SERVES 4

600g (1lb 5oz) cooked new potatoes cut into 1.5cm (½ inch) chunks

3 spring onions, finely chopped

1 tbsp finely chopped chives

1 tbsp finely chopped parsley

1 tbsp finely chopped mint

½ tsp sea salt flakes

4–5 tbsp Magic Mayonnaise – see page 27 (or any mayonnaise of choice)

salt and pepper, to taste

Place the potatoes into a roomy mixing bowl, add all of the ingredients and stir to combine. Transfer to a presentation dish and serve.

TIME FOR FRIENDS

The one headache for me when it comes to spending time with beloved family and friends is gift-buying ideas. My close friends from years ago now have a get-together at birthdays – a drink and a chat – rather than get hung up on buying gifts for each other.

That said, I do love to give something home-made, and that can be a cake, sweets, biscuits or even a simple plant cutting in a pretty pot, or a beeswax wrap or two made from cotton remnants – the possibilities are endless.

GIFT BOX

Have you ever made a gift box? Just a little one, but it's a fantastic idea for wedding favours, table gifts at Christmas, a container for recycled soap (see page 93), or to use to give a piece of wedding or Christmas cake.

You just need two square pieces of paper – no glue, staples or cutting. Use upcycled gift wrap, biodegradable paper or just white paper if you prefer – you can colour it if you like, or get the children involved to decorate.

You will need

2 sheets of paper: one 20cm (8in) square and the other 21cm (8¼ inches) square

The smaller piece will be the base and the larger one the lid. Start with the smaller square sheet, folding in half to create a rectangle and then in half again widthways to a square. Run your fingernail firmly along each fold as these lines will become your guides. Open out the sheet.

Fold each of the four corner points into the centre, using the creases you just made as a guide to ensure the resulting shape is an exact square. Reinforce the folds with your fingernail to create neat sharp lines, as before.

With the paper still folded, fold the right edge into the centre of the square and the left edge in to meet it along the centre line. Reinforce the creases and unfold them. Repeat with the top and bottom edges.

Open the top and bottom triangular folds. Lift the two longer sides on the right and left so that they face each other, vertically. Take one of the pointed edges and fold the point up and over, using the crease marks you made earlier to tuck in the two sides of each edge and create a side of the box, returning the point of the triangle back to the centre. Repeat on the other side to form the base box.

Set the base to one side then do exactly the same with the slightly larger piece of paper. The lid will then sit over the base perfectly.

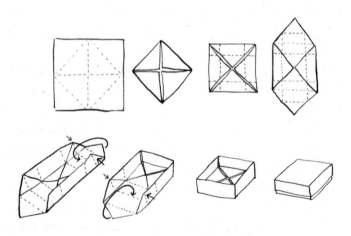

GIFT WRAP

Gift wrapping and greetings cards have become big business, and it seems that every year a new trend appears with bigger and bigger bows, ribbons and glitter – huge, glitter-laden cards and those balloons are even worse. Apart from the expense, their life is brief. The cards may be on display for a week or so but the wrapping – oh dear, the wrapping, plastic tape and ribbon is ripped up upon receipt and enjoyed for just a few seconds before ending its life in landfill.

Glitter and balloons, of course, are plastic, wrapping tape the same, and the shiny finish on lots of gift wrap, ribbons and the like belongs in the same club. None of it easily degrades, creating millions of tons of waste – most of which ends up in landfill.

Many years ago, when my children were small, I used to save all of the Christmas and greetings cards, give them each a pair of plastic scissors and on rainy days they would cut out and paste them as new cards. Taking this a step further, I now keep all of the cards, use a pair of pinking shears and a hole punch and cut them into gift tags threaded with string that will be reused the next Christmas or for birthdays.

At the time of writing I have just invested in a roll of biodegradable brown paper, a ball of jute compostable string and brown eco-friendly paper tape. I am not going to buy any more gift wrap, tags or bows. I have finished wrapping a little gift for my granddaughter. Wrapped in brown paper, tied off with string and sealed with paper tape. It has two labels – one is a brown paper label that advises that all of the packaging should go into the compost bin and the other label is a home 'cut-out' from one of my birthday cards. It is bright pink and I have written her name on it.

The 'icing on the cake' for this parcel is a tiny posy of dried buttercups, wrapped in pink paper ribbon (see page 111 on drying flowers). It looks so beautiful, individual, and is not costing our Earth!

The 100-metre roll of paper will last me for years, I am sure, as will the string and the tape. I cannot wait to get going on Christmas gift wrap using small cones, holly sprigs, ivy, cinnamon sticks, dried orange slices, etc. – exciting!

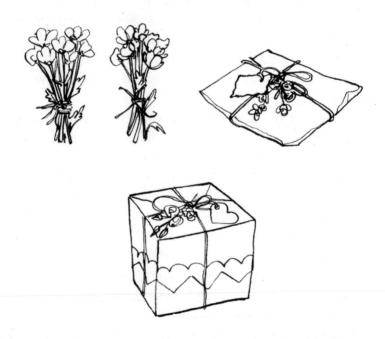

BEESWAX WRAPS

Beeswax wraps are easy to make, cost about a quarter of the ones that you can buy, can persuade your plastic-wrap-loving friends to think again about single-use plastic and will upcycle those odds and sods of remnant cotton you may have, or be a great upcycle project for any pieces of cotton clothing no longer worn.

I was certainly the 'cling film queen' – I loved it and used metres of it. Wrapping sandwiches, vegetables, cheese, pastry for resting, bread for proving, bowls of hot and cold food – you name it, it probably had single-use cling film around it. I then realized, for the sake of our planet and in a move to reduce my household waste, that I needed to change. After all, I can actually remember the days when cling film didn't exist, so all I needed to do was have a think.

Beeswax wraps, pieces of pretty cotton fabric in various sizes, coated on both sides in beeswax that can be used to wrap food items such as sandwiches, herbs and so on, are now hitting the market at an alarming rate and at premium prices. They can be used to freeze food, can be washed, refreshed and they last for ages. They can be expensive – unless you make them yourself.

You will need

    very thin 100 per cent cotton (polyester blends give grainy results and are not biodegradable)

    lipped oven tray (use an old one or line with reusable baking parchment so that the solid unused wax can be peeled off and stored for another time) beeswax pellets – 100g (3½oz) will make 4–6 wraps

pinking shears

2 pairs or tongs or tweezers, or rubber gloves

Preheat the oven to 180°C/375°F/gas 4. Cut your fabric into squares or circles – squares are better for wrapping foods, circles make great pot covers. Make one wrap at a time. Lay the cotton flat on the baking sheet then scatter over a good handful of beeswax. Don't worry about how much to use, the fabric will only absorb what it needs.

Pop the tray into the oven for around 2 minutes or until you see the beeswax has melted and looks like oil. Take the tray from the oven and, using gloved hands, tweezers or tongs, lift the fabric from the wax and allow any surplus to drain off back onto the tray.

Continue to hold the fabric above the tin for a minute or two and very quickly the fabric will cool down and the wax will set. That's it – you have your own beeswax wrap. Once stiff, set aside and continue making your next wrap, adding a few more beeswax pellets each time.

Any wax left in the base of your tin after making your wraps should be left to set, then just scraped or lifted off and popped back into your bag of wax to reuse later. Never be tempted to pour it down the sink.

Your wraps can be washed in hand-warm soapy water (but not so hot that the wax begins to melt) and air dried. After a time they will crease from usage but they can be quickly refreshed by simply laying them back onto the baking tray with a little extra beeswax and into the oven for a minute or so. The creases will be gone, leaving it refreshed and looking as good as new. When your beeswax wraps have seen better days, they can be tossed onto the compost heap.

LAVENDER BAGS

I think lavender bags are making a comeback! When I was small old ladies and women teachers used to smell of lavender and I realize now it was probably their clothes. Back in the days before polyester, nylon and other manmade fibres, clothes made of natural silk, wool and cotton could be attacked by moth larvae. If clothes moths find your best 100 per cent angora sweater, they can lay their eggs on it, then the tiny grubs nibble small holes in the fibres. I remember small polo-shaped, pungent-smelling moth balls used to be hung in wardrobes on lengths of twine – until they were banned because the chemical used was found to be a health hazard to humans.

As with many problems, prevention is better than cure. Clothes moths will seek out dark places that are not disturbed, so to keep my woollens safe I move them from time to time and in each drawer or hanging space I place a lavender bag. A whiff of lavender is a great deterrent and will send the egg-laying female moth flying off somewhere else.

I have seen lavender bags for sale for silly prices when they are so easily made at home. As well as the insect-repelling properties, lavender will freshen your car, wardrobes and drawers and items of clothing will smell divine. I think these little bags make great gifts, too.

I find making a heart shape is quicker and easier than making a square or an actual bag – less work and a great gift idea. The easiest way to make bags (by hand or machine) is to cut a heart-shaped bag about 15cm (6 inches) wide. This is a great upcycle for scraps and remnants of material.

You will need

colourful cotton remnants – two pieces each around 18cm
  (7 inches) square per bag
pencil or tailor's chalk (Or mark using a soap sliver, see page 93)
pinking shears
needles and sewing thread (machine or hand)
buttons
approximately 10–12g (½oz) dried lavender
lengths of ribbon – about 20cm (8 inches) per bag
bright button (optional)

See the tips on drying flowers on page 111. The method for drying lavender is the same. The flowers on my plants are flourishing in July and I simply pick a bunch, tie with string and hang upside down in a dry place. Once dry to the touch, after a week or so the scented blooms can be easily stripped from the stalk into a paper bag and kept until ready to use.

To make the bags, it is easier to cut out a heart shape if the fabric is folded in half first and pressed, then use a pencil or tailor's chalk to draw a 'half heart'. Use pinking shears to cut out, then open out to achieve a perfect shape. Cutting out a double piece of fabric at the same time will give a perfect match. Use pinking shears for cutting out to prevent fraying.

With wrong sides together and patterned side facing out, sew the two pieces together, about 5mm (¼ inch) in from the edge. Neat stitches are guaranteed by machine and if sewing by hand, use a back stitch. Leave a gap at the heart's cleavage (I don't know what else to call it!) about 2.5cm (1 inch) wide so that once finished you can pop the end of a small funnel into the hole and fill up the heart with dried lavender. Don't fill too full, allow space to close up the two pieces of fabric and to be able to move the lavender around freely in the bag.

Sew up the opening, enclosing at the same time a bow and loop of ribbon for hanging. I then finish with a bright button which will cover up the join, look as though it is supporting the ribbon and finishes off the bag beautifully.

TIME TO CLEAN

My green cleaning journey continues, and while my previous book *Clean & Green* is devoted to cleaning tips, home-made product recipes and hints for adopting an eco-friendly lifestyle, since making the switch I am constantly finding new shortcut and eco-friendly swaps. So here I have a number of new recipes and tips to share.

CREAM CLEANER

I write with huge enthusiasm about the many cleaning uses for bicarbonate of soda; I love it, but so much so that I find myself fairly heavy handed with it, using far more than is actually necessary. A sprinkle around to clean the sink, the teapot, remove scuffs and marks on paintwork and white shoes is all that is necessary, yet my approach was overdosing to the extreme.

I have discovered that making up a quantity of my cream cleaner helps the bicarbonate of soda to go further, and last longer because less is needed. Having a blob on a cloth goes straight to the spot, no waste or spills, and it is more effective than dry bicarbonate of soda on its own.

The three main ingredients are all gentle cleansers but when mixed together to a cream are even more amazing. My cream cleaner is perfect for granite worktops and sanitary ware, being non-acidic and only slightly abrasive. It works a treat and many followers sing its praises over commercial cream cleaning, plastic-packaged products.

You will need

200g (7oz) bicarbonate of soda
70ml (3oz) vegetable glycerine
20ml (1¼fl oz) eco-friendly washing-up liquid
a few drops essential oil for perfume (optional)
500ml (14fl oz) jar or tub

Simply place all the ingredients into the jar or tub, stir to a thick smooth paste and it is ready to use. When making my first batch, I poured it into a reused plastic squeezy bottle, but I found that the cleaner was not free-flowing enough to run to the bottom of the bottle when nearly empty, so I now find a jar is much better and it has its own mini wooden spoon kept inside for stirring and dispensing.

Adding more glycerine or washing-up liquid to make the cleaner thinner just caused it to split. Commercial products use 'surfactants' to emulsify ingredients which prevent this happening – some of these mystery chemicals are eco-friendly, others, however, are not!

Very recently I made an amazing discovery. I have a stripped-pine kitchen table, 40 years old and bought back in the 1970s when pine was 'the thing'. This table stains easily and about once a week, before going green, I used to scrub it with chlorine bleach! The table looked a bit dull and lifeless but was clean and stain-free. Trying to apply polish or coconut oil to give it a lift just made it very sticky.

Now I give it a rub over with a sprinkle of bicarbonate of soda, wipe it with a warm cloth and that's it. Except for, have you guessed? I cleaned it with cream cleaner – about 2 table-spoons – then rubbed this in with a loofah scourer, using just enough warm water to spread it around. Taking just a warm damp cloth I wiped away the cream cleaner, thinking it looked great. I returned to the table some hours later and couldn't believe my eyes. The table had dried, felt silky smooth but had taken on a rich golden colour I'd not seen since it was new decades ago.

The cream cleaner seemingly has hidden powers. The bicarbonate of soda cleans and gently rubs away stains, the washing-up liquid, while assisting with the cleaning, also emulsifies the ingredients, and the vegetable glycerine, as well as having gentle cleaning properties (it is used in many skin products), obviously treats and feeds the wood, leaving it looking so beautiful.

I can't tell you how happy it has made me. The colour doesn't fade, the surface remains silky and non-sticky and I clean the table the same way now every week.

Silver Cleaning

I must share this little tip. My friend has an antique silver pepper pot, been in their family for many years. As I am always ranting on about the toxic chemicals contained in many metal-cleaning products she asked me to clean this item, explaining how precious it was, it mustn't get scratched and she definitely didn't want to get the green felt base to get wet.

I reached for the cream cleaner and two cloths. A gentle rub over with a dry cloth dipped in cream cleaner immediately removed the tarnish – the cloth became stained with black, no scratching and no wetting. The second cloth I used to give a final buff and polish, and there is an added bonus: the vegetable glycerine leaves a light coating, which slows down future tarnish.

My cream cleaner is now my go-to for those precious items or very large items unsuitable for dipping. Photo frames, large trays, glass items with silver trims – it does a sterling job!

Red wine-stained floor grouting

A red-wine spill on a tiled floor shouldn't pose a problem, I thought. A quick wipe and the tile is clean and stain-free. However, the next day, when all was thoroughly dried, I had a residual black stain to the white grouting that had refused to budge. In the old days I would have reached for the chlorine bleach to instantly remove the stain, but chlorine bleach has been banned from my shopping list for some years now. You've guessed it – my cream cleaner comes to the rescue!

A blob applied directly to the stain, rubbed in with an old toothbrush, left for only a minute or two then wiped off and the stain was completely gone.

Grease

The beast when it comes to grease! I have an outside kitchen – sounds grand, but it is simply a hob outside in a covered area, and it is brilliant when it comes to frying. Splashing, spitting and cooking smells are kept outside, which is ideal when cooking fish.

The area does get greasy, though, because being outside, dirt flying around sticks to greasy bits and the whole thing soon becomes unsightly. Cream cleaner, with its light abrasive texture, cuts through the dirt and grease perfectly and is probably better than any commercial equivalent.

White Trainers and Sports Shoes

A damp cloth dipped in cream cleaner and rubbed over scuff marks and smudges on sports shoes will clean them in minutes.

The trainers or sports shoes now look pristine, but what about the white laces? Pop them into an old cup or beaker, add a tablespoon of washing soda and 1 teaspoon of green bleach (sodium percarbonate, see page 240), cover with just-boiled water and leave for an hour. The laces can then be taken from the water, rinsed in cold water and air-dried. The whitening solution can then be used to swish around the sink to whiten it too.

SUEDE AND NUBUCK CLEANER

I have a pair of turquoise suede shoes that I love, and when they were new I was very careful with them, but by their second summer I was wearing them in all weathers. In the garden, out in the rain, they were worn in the kitchen when cooking, and you can guess – they became very grubby indeed. So much so I had thought them destined for the bin.

Proprietary suede and nubuck cleaning products can be quite pricey, often come in aerosol form, with lots of packaging, and these shoes really didn't warrant the financial or planetary expense. I decided to have a go at cleaning the grease splashes, water marks and general grubbiness and was delighted with the results.

You will need

- a cloth dampened with water
- 1 tbsp bicarbonate of soda
- 1 tbsp eco-friendly washing-up liquid mixed to a paste with 1 tbsp bicarb
- a stiff brush – a suede shoe brush or small, hard-bristle nail brush

Start by dabbing the dampened cloth in the dry bicarbonate of soda and work this around the shoes, rubbing quite vigorously. Be sure to cover the whole shoe in the process, otherwise you will be left with obvious untreated areas.

Then mix the paste using 1 tablespoon of bicarbonate of soda and eco-friendly washing-up liquid. Using the damp cloth, rub this in, making your way around the whole shoe, paying particular attention to the water-marked areas and the grease spots and stains.

Don't be concerned if the shoes look worryingly dark-coloured after this; mine did even though I knew they had not got wet. Use a clean, damp cloth to wipe over the whole shoe, making sure to cover every part of it with a thin layer of the paste. Leave to dry outside, or in a well-ventilated area, for several hours.

Once dried, use the stiff brush to work vigorously at the shoes, removing powdery residue and brushing up the suede.

NOTE: Bicarbonate of soda and a damp cloth may be all that is required to clean most footwear, but mine were very dirty and badly stained. I had nothing to lose with my shoes, but I would recommend testing first on an area that is out of sight. Trying to spot-clean the shoes simply created a clean patch, so I have found it necessary to treat the whole shoe for an even look.

FRESHEN-UP VINEGAR

Those of us that have started out on the 'green' cleaning journey will be buying white vinegar as a 'must-have' for the cleaning shelf. It is the effective ingredient in so many of my cleaning recipes, and I love it.

Vinegar kills germs, cuts through grease, is a natural water softener, it destroys limescale, prevents anti-static cling and is therefore perfect as a fabric softener, it dissolves residues left by soaps and detergents, is not expensive and, of course, does not harm our waterways. Some followers tell me they don't, however, like the smell.

I have seen that 5-litre (1-gallon) containers of lemon cleaning vinegar are now available in the shops, and even containers of standard white vinegar labelled as 'cleaning vinegar' are being sold for more than double the price of a supermarket own brand. Buyer beware! Choose standard white distilled vinegar, and if you really don't like the smell it can be improved with a little added fragrance.

You will need

potato peeler
1 spent lemon (that you have used in baking or cooking) or
   1 whole lemon
1 litre (34fl oz) glass jar with non-corrosive lid
lemon juicer
750ml (25fl oz) white vinegar

You can, of course, use a whole lemon for this recipe but it's also a fantastic way of getting the most out of spent lemons before adding them to the compost bin. Use the lemon juicer to extract as much juice as possible and add to the jar along with the spent halves.

If using an unused lemon, use the potato peeler to pare away thick strips from the lemon rind and place these in the jar. Cut the lemon in half then use the juicer to extract as much juice as possible and add it to the jar.

Pour over the white vinegar and cover with a non-corrosive lid. Leave on the shelf for about a week or so before using in your favourite cleaning recipes (adds a gorgeous scent to fabric conditioner, see page 251). When using, I tend decant the lemon vinegar into a different bottle, straining out any lemon pulp, and then top up the vinegar in the original jar several times before discarding the lemon altogether after a number of weeks.

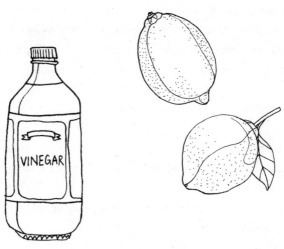

PURE MAGIC

This excellent eco-friendly product takes pride of place in my book *Clean & Green,* and while developing the recipe certainly gave me the run around, it really does what it says on the tin. It is magic!

I have decided to repeat the recipe only because I love it and there may be some readers that haven't made up a bottle yet and, because it is SO good, a re-brand was necessary, which takes it to another level. I asked my followers to get involved in a new name, and from September 2021 it was elevated from Toilet Magic to Pure Magic!

I really do urge you to try it. I've found so many more uses since I first developed this recipe. Cheaper than branded eco-friendly products, it has so many uses and, of course, there's no single-use plastic packaging.

I used to be a chlorine bleach addict – squirting it freely down the sink, down the toilet, down every drain, to whiten whites, scrub grouting – it was my go-to germ killer and whitener. Then I read the back label, the small print and hazard data sheets and understood how damaging it is to the environment. It takes years and years to break down, is toxic and the fumes can irritate the eyes, throat, lungs and skin.

Pure Magic is not harmful, it kills germs, destroys limescale (which bleach alone doesn't do) and smells fresh. It takes minutes to make and doesn't deteriorate once mixed. I now make two bottles at a time.

You will need

200g (7oz) citric acid
150ml (5fl oz) just-boiled water
20ml (¾fl oz) eco-friendly washing-up liquid
10 drops organic tea tree oil (you can omit for non-toilet cleaning) or other scent of choice
400ml (14fl oz) spray bottle

Place the measured crystals in a heatproof measuring jug and pour over just-boiled water. Stir until the liquid is clear and the crystals have dissolved, then simply add the eco-friendly washing-up liquid and tea tree oil and mix well using a small whisk.

Leave the liquid in the jug to cool completely, uncovered, for a few hours to prevent crystallization, then pour into a spray bottle and it is ready to use.

Before I explain the other uses for it besides the loo, I really need to tell you my toilet story – I tell it to all of my friends!

I have what I call the shower toilet, which was such a huge problem. It was badly stained and would only whiten up after a half bottle of bleach was poured down and left for a day or two. Whenever I went on holiday – almost a whole bottle of bleach was left to do its work while I was away. I feel so terrible about this now.

Once white, within a day or so it was badly stained again. I had tried everything, even emptying the water from the bowl and giving it a good scrub – I couldn't shift the stains. I considered that at some time I would need to replace this toilet because I believed the porcelain glaze was damaged and constant staining was inevitable. Here is where the story gets exciting.

Having gone green and no longer using chlorine bleach the toilet clean was changed and I moved over to Toilet Magic. The stains were improved but not completely gone, yet reverting to chlorine bleach was not an option. Then, one morning, after having used Toilet Magic for a week or so, I looked down into the toilet in shock and horror – the toilet was broken. In the base of the bowl was what looked like a dirty broken cup laid on its side in the water. The bowl must be cracked, I thought, something must have been dropped into it. On with my rubber gloves to retrieve this broken object.

Amazingly, what I lifted out of the toilet was a cup-shaped, thick chunk of limescale that had been hugging the base of the toilet bowl for years! My home-made Toilet Magic had resolved a problem that had been around for as long as I could remember. The bowl is now smooth, white, shiny and never, ever stains.

I now mix 'Pure' Magic and use it in different ways. Some goes into a spray bottle for use in the toilet (remember to rinse the nozzle after use to prevent it seizing from the sticky citric acid), then I mix a solution and keep it in a screw-topped bottle to use for other jobs.

I am often asked, 'Why not use Toilet Magic as an all-purpose cleaner all around the house?' While it is a great cleaner it also has a downside; if it is not rinsed thoroughly it will dry sticky and, secondly, it can leave white smears (as the citric acid crystallizes). I found this out to my cost when I considered it would be a great floor cleaner. It removed the stains perfectly but then my slippers stuck to the floor and white streaks appeared everywhere as it dried. Pure Magic is a wonder in the right places!

Whiter Whites and Stain removal

Use 2–3 tablespoons of Pure Magic in cold water for an overnight pre-soak of your white washing and to dissolve the most stubborn of stains.

Fixed Stains

I continue to experiment with Pure Magic, and while going through old white t-shirts I discovered a number had found their way to the bottom of the drawer, because they each had a fixed stain from goodness knows when. With nothing to lose, I decided to give them a treatment.

This little tip has been used by many followers with great results. I have used it on cotton and polyester.

Use a small paintbrush to dampen the stain with Pure Magic – I have found that if the garment is already slightly damp this is easier to do. Add a sprinkle of table salt and massage together to a gritty paste using the paintbrush. Pop the article in a plastic bag (a used one) to keep everything moist. Leave for an hour or two – or even overnight – then remove the item from the bag and pop it into the washing machine set at 20°C (yes, 20°C! See pages 246-250), along with another load.

This little tip will remove rust stains from fabric, and a squirt of Pure Magic with salt rubbed over will also remove rust from other surfaces.

Two-minute Supersaver – Quick Sink Clean

Pour 1 tablespoon or so of Pure Magic into the sink then scrub around for the quickest clean, stain removal and sanitization of the sink, rinsing well after use.

Dishwasher Clean

To obtain the best performance from your dishwasher, a regular clean and maintenance check is necessary. I was shocked when I saw proprietary cleaning products on the supermarket shelf at around £3 per use, promising to clean and freshen the machine and remove limescale.

The clean can be done at home for a fraction of the price, with no plastic packaging and no harmful chemicals.

You will need

an old toothbrush or small kitchen brush
hot soapy water
100g (3½oz) citric acid crystals or 100ml (3½fl oz) Pure Magic

Try to remember to check the machine's filter about once a month. To do this, unscrew the filter cover – mine comes away in three parts. There is the large plate cover with a basket inside and then a finer mesh basket inside of that. If not attended to the filter can become clogged with food debris, grease and then, at its worst, is unable to clean dishes effectively and the machine starts to smell offensive.

Use hot soapy water to scrub each element then rinse them under the tap. Replace everything.

Secondly, check the salt dispenser and make sure the levels are topped up. A dishwasher in need of salt will produce cloudy, dull glassware. Finally, to give the dishwasher a thorough wash, cleanse, descale and freshen up, either add 100g (3½oz) citric acid crystals straight into the machine or pour in 100ml (3½fl oz) Pure Magic, whichever is the most convenient to you.

Your machine will be sparkling, fresh, free of limescale and efficient.

Plant Pots

This was another surprise find. I adore terracotta pots and I came across three small 7.5cm (3 inch) ones in the shed. They were years old, bought well before their plastic counterparts hit the market. One was slightly chipped, and all three were badly stained on the inside and the outside. Green algae had turned black over time, water-scale marks, debris and an all-over dirty feel. I decided because they were so beautiful I would try to clean them up. Warm soapy water was used to scrub off the surplus muck, but sadly old staining was still present.

Before going to bed I popped them into clean hot water with a squirt of eco-friendly washing-up liquid and 2–3 tablespoons of Pure Magic and left them overnight. I couldn't contain my excitement the next morning – natural cleaning has this effect on me!

The lightest of a rub with an old toothbrush and these pots were like new. The glaze was smooth and shiny again. Who would have known? I would never have considered these pots suitable for indoor use but they are now special. I added a little acrylic paint in the form of simple flowers, mainly to cover up chips, and they now sit on my windowsill growing baby cuttings. (See page 293 for how to take cuttings.)

Further Experiments

I have used a spray of Pure Magic to successfully clean so many things. My green algae-covered outside drain, a stone birdbath, slippery steps, a squirt onto badly stained areas of my coffee machine. I encourage you to try it for yourself, but always spot-test on a small area of whatever you're cleaning first.

CITRIC ACID

As a cleaning product, citric acid can be used in varying dilutions, saving money and packaging on specific products.

Shower Heads

Even the toughest of limescale problems can be treated quickly and easily using citric acid. I make up a solution of one-part citric acid to four-parts boiling water, and once the liquid is clear and has cooled down I use it to descale the shower head by unscrewing it and soaking it in the liquid for an hour or so.

Coffee Machines

Instead of buying descaling solution, make your own using 1 tablespoon of citric acid dissolved in 500ml (18fl oz) boiling water, then once clear and cooled down, use to clean and descale your machine.

Shower Screens (glass or plastic)

I have had so many questions about shower screens, including before and after photos of troublesome screens which have become badly stained with hard-water marks, soap scum, calcium deposits, lime and rust. Citric acid does a sterling job on all these.

You will need

Pure Magic, if you have it made up, or make a smaller quantity:
75ml (3fl oz) just-boiled water
100g (3½oz) citric acid
Pyrex jug and spoon
5ml eco-friendly washing-up liquid
funnel
300ml (10fl oz) spray bottle (reuse a plastic one)
exfoliating gloves

Pour the just-boiled water over the citric acid in the jug, stir, then add the washing-up liquid and once clear leave to cool. Transfer to the bottle then spray all over the troubled areas. I find exfoliating gloves excellent for the next step: they have just enough abrasion without any scratch. Using your gloved hands, rub around the mark in a circular motion. The solution will froth a little. When you have covered all areas, leave for 15–20 minutes for it to do its work.

Rinse off with warm water and make sure you do it well because the concentrated citric acid solution will dry sticky. The shower screen will be restored to its former glory.

MOULD ON FABRICS

Mould spots can be found all over the house following winter months of condensation build-up, especially in kitchens and steamy bathrooms. In many areas they can be easily wiped away but on fabrics they can be troublesome.

Precious items will develop mould if stored in damp places or if they have not been completely dry when put away. I have followers who have sent me screenshots of garden cushions, a picnic basket and a child's pram hood, spotted with mould that went on to be cleaned up using the above method.

A concerned follower sent over an image of a dark grey vertical blind with hefty mould spots along the bottom. Knowing that citric acid will kill mould I suggested a light spray using the citric acid mix, then a light scrub using an old toothbrush, a clean water rinse followed by air drying. She was absolutely delighted – blinds refreshed. Worked a treat!

RUST ON FABRICS

Rust stains can present on fabrics, especially around zips and fasteners if the item has been allowed to get wet then not dried thoroughly or was packed away when damp. This can happen particularly on items such as garden soft furnishings – zips on outdoor seat cushions, fasteners on picnic baskets, etc.

A follower presented a delicate problem – a vintage wedding dress that had a rust-stained area on the fabric around the zip at the back of the dress. Tentatively, I suggested she unfastened the zip and with the metal facing downwards sprayed over citric acid then rubbed in a little table salt. Leave for several minutes then rinse off with cold water. It is important that the liquid running off passes from the fabric down into the zip to ensure the stain is not carried back into the dress. As with all new problems or precious items, I suggested a test area first.

You can guess, otherwise I wouldn't be offering the same advice again, I was delighted when she sent me before and after photos – the stain and rust had dissolved, the dress was saved and I was very happy. Be extra careful if your item is dry clean only.

'TWO FOR ONE' SUPERSAVER

Limescale if left untreated looks unsightly, is corrosive and can harbour germs. I live in a hard-water area and the kettle very quickly gets a limescale build-up. Popping a couple of spent lemons in the kettle, boiling them up, leaving to stand overnight then pouring away the water is a quick and easy method for keeping on top of things. There are those times when the limescale has been allowed to become too thick and we need more power. After boiling the kettle, stand it in the sink, remove the lid and spoon over 50–80g (2–3oz) citric acid. There will be an immediate fizz and in only a few minutes the limescale will have dissolved. Rather than pour the solution away I then do a few extra jobs with it.

While the solution is still hot, I pour it into a large bowl and add my shower head. I use a pastry brush to apply a little of this solution around the base of taps, around the plughole or anywhere I see a spot of limescale. Pour a little into a deep plastic bottle cap and wrap this around a tap spout using an elastic band or tape to secure. I have even dropped a few pieces of costume jewellery in leftover solution for a quick clean up.

Before finally pouring it down the sink, I will tip it over my dishcloth in the bowl to clean and sanitize. Citric acid kills bacteria, so as well as descaling appliances it is great for general disinfecting and cleaning. A good rinse after soaking and the cloth is fresh and whitened without the need for chlorine bleach.

SODIUM PERCARBONATE – GREEN BLEACH

While on the subject of moving away from chlorine bleach, sodium percarbonate is now my green best friend. It may seem expensive compared to chlorine bleach, but a little goes a long way and it is possible to do more than one job at once.

Green bleach will instantly whiten my teapot and the mesh insert but I pop my dishcloth in at the same time so that I can do two jobs in one. Pop 1–2 teaspoons of green bleach in the base of the teapot, pour over boiling water to fill right to the top, then it's in with my dishcloth. Leave a few minutes then pour away – there's no harm to the waterways. Even the sink and drain get a quick clean.

I also whiten the inside of my enamel cookware using a tablespoon or two of green bleach, then pouring over boiling water and leaving it for an hour or so. I also throw in my dishcloth and loofah scourer at the same time.

SODIUM CARBONATE – WASHING SODA

I use washing soda almost daily and it is a green alternative to so many of the products I used to buy. The toughest burnt-on deposits will lift off following an overnight soak in a cup of washing soda and boiling water.

Once opened, however, if the packet is not kept well sealed the contents can clump together. So, either keep the bag sealed by folding it over and securing it with a clothes peg or transfer the contents of the opened pack into a glass jar and inside this keep a silica sachet – a great upcycling idea for one of those little packs found in a new handbag. The silica gel will absorb moisture and prevent clumping. I keep a sachet in each of my glass jars of dry cleaning ingredients – citric acid, bicarbonate of soda, washing soda and green bleach. Do not use silica packets in any food ingredients.

TWO-MINUTE SUPERSAVER –
OIL AND FAT RESIDUES

Ever wonder what to do with residual fat or oil in a roasting tin or frying pan? Even after it has been poured off into a jar or bottle there is still a coating hanging onto the pan or tin.

Don't ever be tempted to add your oily pan or tin to the washing-up water or, even worse, pour the fat straight down the sink. The combination of flushed solids such as congealed grease, oil and fat mixed with other products such as non-biodegradable wipes form large, rock-like masses of waste matter called fatbergs in drainage pipes. These obviously block drains and sewers and are very costly to remove. Not only are they disgusting and expensive to resolve, they can cause environmental problems when drains get blocked, resulting in sewage overflows which then go on to pollute other waters.

A sprinkling of 2–3 tablespoons of washing soda over the oily pan will soak up the residue so that it can then be scraped off as a lump and discarded. Rather than tipping straight into my non-plastic-lined bin I now discard messy items such as this into an empty paper flour or sugar bag first. The pan has been cleaned of fat and food debris and can be washed in warm soapy water without contaminating the water with fat.

SUSTAINABLE SOAP NUTS

Soapberries or soap nuts are gaining in popularity and are the dried fruit shells harvested from soapberry trees found in warm, tropical climates. They can be expensive and I question the sustainability of a natural product if it has to be transported half way around the world. I can easily make my own version at home with familiar and local 'natural freebie' ingredients.

The dried nuts contain natural soap called saponin which is released when in contact with water, they can be used for up to three washes and are composted after use. Thankfully, conkers (also known as horse chestnuts or buckeyes) contain saponin and do the same thing! The memories I have of walking home from school in the rain as a child and being puzzled at the mass of bubbles on the road as the cars whizzed by squashing the conkers. I now understand why.

Unlike soap nuts, conkers contain the saponin in their flesh rather than the shell so it is necessary to break into the shiny nut to release the soap. I have been making a liquid conker detergent for several years, but due to its short shelf life (it starts to ferment after about a month), I could only use it for part of the year, unless I froze batches, which I have done but it does use up valuable freezer space.

I decided to make Conker 'Sustainable' Soap Nuts and because they keep indefinitely my detergent supply is now free, easy to make and will keep me going all year round.

You will need

500g (1lb 2oz) large fresh conkers
knife
chopping board or powerful blender
dehydrator or oven
baking sheet
2 airtight storage jars
1–2 drops essential oil for perfume

It is important to harvest conkers that are fresh and shiny and as large as possible, so they are easy to slice. This is a seasonal job for me in the UK, best done in September or early October when conkers are in season. Cut the conker in half then, with the cut side down on the board, cut each half into slices (4–5 slices per conker half). Alternatively, if you have a powerful blender the conkers can be blitzed into rough, uneven pieces.

Spread the pieces, shell and flesh together, on a baking sheet and dry in the oven or a dehydrator set at 80°C for about 5 hours or until the pieces are completely dry to the touch and don't stick to your hands. Transfer to an airtight storage jar and add 1–2 drops essential oil to perfume, if required.

These soap nuts can be used for up to three washes.

TO USE

Add 2–3 large tablespoons of the dried pieces to a zip-up laundry bag and into the drum with the laundry. Don't worry that the soap will prevent your clothes from rinsing – the natural properties contained in the detergent soften the water too and less soap is released during cold rinsing.

Between washes, leave the soap nuts in the laundry bag and hang it up so that air can freely circulate, then the nuts can dry out without going mouldy. If you have a plentiful supply of conkers you may choose to use the nuts only once, but I love the fun of seeing suds being produced even on the third wash. I use the nuts for cold washing too (see pages 250–1).

Decorate the jars and give to family and friends as a fun and tempting gift idea to get the green conversation rolling!

LAUNDRY LIFE: COLD WASHING

This has changed my life!

When a US follower asked me my thoughts and views on cold washing I had to admit I drew a blank. I had no views because I didn't know it was a thing. Hot washing, yes, and for much of my life I had believed and understood the hotter the better for the whitest whites, the cleanest of clean and the best all-round wash. A routine colour wash was usually 40°C, a white wash 60°C and tea towels and bath towels a thundering 90°C!

I then went on to read extensively about 'cold washing', and I grabbed any morsel of information I could find to bring myself up to speed on recent developments. With this newfound information (and not so new, to many, as I discovered), I was impatient and excited to have a go myself. I have to say the 20°C cycle on my machine had never been used, and the 30°C cycle very rarely. I used to use a quick 30° wash only for lightly soiled or special and often single garments that were precious but that I couldn't be bothered to hand wash.

I think I could write a whole book about what I now understand about cold washing, but I will make this as succinct as possible and leave you to decide whether it is one you want to try.

Detergent manufacturers have for years been researching and putting products onto the market that are promised to remove stains at lower temperatures. Apparently 'cold washing' as a marketing tool did not hit the spot with consumers other than in Australia, and so it never took off. The concept instead was re-branded and packaged into the promise that stains can be removed even at lower temperatures.

Even though I had seen those adverts, I was not convinced and continued to use 40°, 50°, 60° and 90°C cycles. Even if the garment label stated 30°C, it went into a full bundle and was tossed into the machine at 40° or 50°C.

I was really wanting to get started but then my dilemma – I didn't want to go back to using chemical-heavy synthetic, brightly coloured and perfumed detergents, which I assumed had to be the secret to success.

I had already long since replaced branded detergents with my own blend of natural products yet now was so interested in the concept of a cold wash I had to give it a go. Cold washing, by the way, isn't freezing cold water – the laundry washing temperature is 20 (or 30)°C. I think I prefer to call it 'cool washing'.

The benefits are many. Probably the most significant and immediate benefit is the saving on fuel. Around 90 per cent of the washing machine's use of electricity during its cycle is the heating of the water. Even though a cycle may seem lengthy (my 20°C cycle goes on for 2 hours 13 minutes), the use of the motor to simply turn the drum, lifting and dropping the laundry into a pool of water, uses minimal power. Selecting a 20°C cycle reduces our fuel consumption, which saves money too.

Fabrics are less likely to fade and shrink and will therefore last longer if washed in cold water. Microfibres contained in synthetic and polyester clothing are released in hot water. These then travel into the water  ways as small plastic pollutants which can then be mistaken for food by ocean organisms, and go on to disrupt the eco system. I read that studies showed that during cold washing significantly fewer fibres were released into the water.

Not all stains are water-soluble and using hot water can actually fix a stain into fabric. I know this is the case as blood and grease stains can become permanent if not treated before washing. Cold washing can actually help to remove certain protein stains, and even if there is still evidence of a stain after washing, it will not have fixed and can be treated. There is less chance of limescale build-up as the heating element of the washing machine has less work to do, which will in turn extend the life of your machine.

With this exciting information, I decided to stick with my green laundry cleaning and in addition committed to turning the dial down to just 20°C. I am now a proud 'Green Cool Washer'.

Am I happy? I AM VERY happy and so are many followers who themselves are amazed by their own cleaning success stories!

Before moving to cool washing, I always pre-treated heavy stains anyway. Anything really soiled, greasy or blood-stained, for example, is best attended to early. A pre-soak is really important and will give the best results once you get into the habit. Heavily soiled items will colour the cold soaking water, meaning your wash in clean water in the machine will so much more effective.

As well as whitening, sodium percarbonate (green bleach) will remove stains and sterilize even in cool water, so I add some into my laundry to whiten and shift marks, along with sodium carbonate (washing soda), which softens the water and has its own stain-dissolving qualities. Hard water if not softened can toughen fabrics.

Adding in my soap nuts or a plant-based liquid soap and my own fabric conditioner (see page 251) – I now feel I have upped my game and am consuming much less electricity, not polluting the waterways, saving money, keeping my washing machine clean and free from limescale, which will prolong its life and at the same time that of my garments.

I hold my hands up and confess that there have been occasions when I have put the washing machine on for just one item – and when I had teenagers they had a fondness for throwing in one garment because they wanted to wear it later that day! I was astounded to read that some washing machines use 150 litres of water per cycle, with the more modern, efficient models now consuming around 50 litres – though that is still a lot! Front-loaders are more efficient than top-loaders because they pick the clothes up and drop them into a limited pool of water, whereas top loaders have the laundry swimming around in a much larger amount. I now think twice before putting the machine on for less than a decent load. Okay, I'll stop now. I think I need to wind this paragraph up before I get carried away.

Have a go, it is working for me, and this is my standard day-to-day recipe for cold washing.

Pre-wash Stain Treatment and Sterilizing

Treat stains before washing with a 1-hour or overnight soak with 100ml (3fl oz) white vinegar or 2 tablespoons of Pure Magic (see page 228) mixed into 300ml (10floz) cold water.

To dissolve stains in more than one item, put them in a bucket of tepid water with a cup of washing soda (sodium carbonate) and leave for 1 hour or, better, overnight.

Some highly soiled or contaminated items might need sterilizing before washing; I use this mix for pre-soaking toilet-cleaning cloths or items that may have been worn or used during an illness, such as diarrhoea and vomiting.

Put 10–15g (about 1 tablespoon) of sodium percarbonate in a large heatproof bowl and pour over a kettle of boiling water to activate it. Top up with hand-hot or cold water, submerge the garments or cloths and soak for 2 hours or overnight.

For any soiled bedding or towels that you are wanting to sterilize following an illness, use a cycle of 60°C or above to disinfect and kill germs.

After pre-treating heavily soiled or stained laundry, remove it from the soaking water, wring out surplus water then wash using a cold wash cycle (I use 20°C) using either of these two blends:

Whites

1–2 tsp sodium percarbonate (green bleach), depending on light or heavy soiling

4 tbsp washing soda crystals (sodium carbonate)

30ml (1fl oz) plant-based liquid soap or 2–3 tbsp Sustainable Soap Nuts (see page 243)

Colours/Dark

1 tsp sodium percarbonate (optional)
4 tbsp washing soda crystals (sodium carbonate)
30ml (1fl oz) plant-based liquid soap or 2–3 tbsp Sustainable
    Soap Nuts (see page 243)

Then add some home-made fabric conditioner/softener:

200ml (7fl oz) white vinegar or Freshen-up Vinegar (see page 226)
15ml (1 tbsp) vegetable glycerine
10 drops organic essential oil (try a flowery one such as ylang
    ylang or lily of the valley)

Add 2–3 tablespoons to the fabric softener compartment for
each wash.

Grease, food and other stains

Fruit juice, food stains, grass stains – an overnight soak in a
bowl of cold water with white vinegar added will work wonders. I usually go with one-part vinegar to three-parts water
and use a small bowl when I only have one item to soak.

Alternatively, a bowl of cold water with 2 tablespoons of Pure Magic will dissolve stains (see page 228 for recipe).

Black Jeans

Many of us possess a favourite pair of black jeans, yet even when strict attention is paid to the wash label, those precious favourite jeans soon seem to take on a grey tinge and are then replaced by a new pair. In my bid to try to buy fewer new clothes, I decided my last new black jeans would receive the best attention and I would endeavour to keep them black as black.

Before their first ever wash, turn the jeans inside out then soak them overnight in a bowl of cold water with a cup of white vinegar added. Vinegar will fix dye to fabrics. There is information that suggests adding salt too, though I have not found that necessary, plus, I use salt as a whitener, so I will keep it well away from my black jeans.

When ready to wash, either pop them into the washing machine on a 20° or 30° cycle or, and I prefer this approach, wash them in lukewarm water by hand using a small amount of plant-based liquid soap – around 1–2 tablespoons. I find a half-hour soak rather than an agitated wash is better on the fabric and the colour. Rinse in cold water then give them a final rinse in a bowl of cold water with a tablespoon of home-made fabric conditioner added (see page 251).

If the weather is fine, let them drip dry outside. If this is not practicable then a very short spin is all that is required. A fast spin has, in the past, left me with permanent 'spin' creases on black jeans, especially low-quality ones. Leave the jeans to dry then either fold neatly or press inside out. I prefer line-drying outside but as with all dark colours, dry out of (bleaching) direct sunlight and turned inside out.

If the jeans are to be washed in the machine then be careful there are no colours in with them that may leave fluff on your perfect black jeans. Better still, don't wash them as often. A blow on the line will do an amazing job of freshening them up without having to launder.

This story never ceases to bring a smile to my face. When my children were teenagers their tendency was to wear a pair of jeans just the once and then put them in the wash. I even recall one time when my daughter was getting ready to go out – she tried on a pair of jeans, walked around in them for about half an hour, had a chat with a friend who said she would be wearing a dress not jeans, then decided against wearing them and tossed them into the laundry basket!

As any parent of teenagers knows, there is absolutely no point entering into what will most certainly become a heated discussion about the excess use of electricity, water, wear and tear on the jeans, more work for me, etc. Instead, unbeknown to them both, I used to take the jeans from the wash basket, inspect them for any spills or stains, turn them inside out, peg them onto the washing line for an hour to freshen up, to then bring them inside for a quick press and back into the cupboard. They never knew – they do now!

Reviving Faded Cotton

I have a quick fix for black cotton items that have gone grey in the wash. I have two black cotton vests and I had popped one into a colours wash. The black vest came out a grey/blue colour and next to my black one looked quite forlorn. I used the method below to revive it.

Take a small bowl, fold the cotton item into it then pour over the strongest black coffee. The coffee needs to be fresh-brewed and hot, not instant. Leave the garment submerged in the coffee overnight, covering it with a plate to keep it in the liquid. The following day, with gloved hands – because it will stain – pour off the coffee and continue to rinse using cold water until the water runs clear. Rinse in a bowl of water and fabric conditioner (see page 251) and then after a final rinse clean, leave to drip-dry outside in the shade. My vest was returned to its former glory.

I have tried this quick natural dyeing on polyester materials with limited success – the fabric needs to be natural cotton.

STUBBORN BLOOD STAINS

Tackling blood stains is often a panic event and many know they can be difficult to remove. But rather than reach for biological detergents, stain-removing sprays or bleach, the following natural stain removal will work wonders.

A fresh stain is easy to deal with and should be submerged immediately in cold water, but more often blood stains are dry by the time the item is ready to be laundered.

Having a bottle of cold salt water at the ready is worth its weight in gold. If you do, it means you can deal with the problem quickly and effectively. Popping a blood stain straight into the washing machine will fix it in place permanently. If you do have a fixed problem such as this, see page 231, which should help.

Making a clear salt-water solution is not straightforward. My initial thoughts were to put salt into a heatproof jug then pour over boiling water, give it a stir and it will dissolve. Not true – I tried it, and while some salt dissolves, there are still grains swirling around, eventually settling at the bottom of the jug.

The secret is to add the salt to the water – little by little and make sure one lot has dissolved before adding more. I make a fairly concentrated solution using 50g (2oz) table salt to 250ml (8fl oz) boiling water.

Place the water in a heatproof jug and add a teaspoon of salt, stir it around and when the water has cleared, add another teaspoon and keep going until all of the salt is dissolved and the water is clear. When it has cooled, transfer to a bottle, label it and pop onto the shelf.

Next time a blood stain needs to be dealt with, simply transfer a little of the solution into a small bowl and submerge the stained area into it. There is no need to use lots of the solution, just enough to cover the stain. Leave for an hour or so and the stain should dissolve.

Blood stains can occur on mattresses and a pad soaked in this solution and dabbed onto the stain will eventually dissolve and lift it. Never use hot water on a blood stain.

I'VE SHRUNK MY JUMPER!

I have done this many times over the years and many a jumper has sadly ended its days due to my mismanagement. The label may have told me this jumper is okay to machine wash or I have been in a rush and it got thrown in with other garments, or I may have been too lazy to hand wash. The end result is that the jumper comes out looking milled up and – well – small!

This method has come to my rescue many times, though I have to say if the woollen garment is terribly shrunk it may not. It has rescued my black polo neck sweater and his expensive cable knit, which I am very relieved that 'him indoors' never knew about.

You will need

a large bowl
the shrunken jumper
hair conditioner
2 tbsp white vinegar
2 large 'bath-size' clean dry towels

In a bowl large enough to take the woollen jumper when folded, give 2–3 squirts of hair conditioner and add the vinegar then fill with lukewarm water. Fold the woollen jumper neatly in the way they do in the shops, with the sides and sleeves folded to the inside, the bottom folded up and the neck folded over the top, finishing in a square shape. The folding will ensure that the jumper can easily fit into the bowl.

Lay the folded jumper onto the bowl of water. No need to submerge it – leave it to absorb the water in its own time and sink to the bottom of the bowl, then leave overnight. The vinegar and hair conditioner will soften the woollen fibres, making them lax and pliable.

The next day, pour the water off the jumper and gently squeeze it to remove the excess. Do not rinse, wring or spin. Lay a large clean towel onto a flat surface (a large table, worktop or a clean floor) and on top place the very wet jumper. Gently pull at it lengthways and sideways, stretching the fibres as you go. Shape the jumper at the shoulder and sleeves, pulling down from shoulder to bottom welt, one hand at the top and one at the bottom. Take your time in gently remoulding your favourite jumper to its original size and shape.

Once you are satisfied that it looks as it used to, take the towel and start rolling from the bottom, nice and tight, until the jumper is concealed in a huge towel and jumper sausage. Rolling tightly will extract much of the remaining moisture. When the towel feels quite wet, unroll and transfer the jumper to the second towel, which again has been laid out on a flat surface.

Arrange the jumper to a 'jumper' shape on the dry towel, again gently pulling and stretching and making sure the welt is straight, the neck even, the sleeves the same length and then just leave it to dry as it is.

It may take some time but don't be tempted to pop it into the dryer or lay it over a radiator, or other heat source, or hang it on the line. Leave to dry completely flat. Your jumper once dried will feel soft and stretchy once more and can be saved from landfill or donation to the charity shop.

HAIR DYE STAINS

Why would you ever go the hairdresser for that much-needed hair colouring wearing a white collared shirt? I did, and hadn't given thought to my dye-stained collar until I took it off that night. It really was unsightly and, I thought, ruined. But here's how to shift that stain.

You will need

a small bowl
100ml (3½fl oz) white vinegar
200ml (7fl oz) cold water

Simply make up a solution of one-part vinegar to two-parts water – 300ml (10fl oz) was sufficient for my blouse. Soak overnight then wash at 20°C as normal. The vinegar will loosen the toughest of stains.

BICARB PASTE

Bicarbonate of soda, one of my green cleaning staples, sometimes need a little something to make it that bit better. I have found that making a paste using equal parts bicarb and eco-friendly washing-up liquid creates a creamy paste which is perfect for dealing with all kinds of stains, particularly oil and grease. In addition to oil spills on clothing, the paste will successfully tackle the following.

Sun Cream, Fake Tan and Makeup Stains

Many people opt for a tanned look, especially over the summer months, and fake tan is a popular way to achieve a golden glow.

While it may look great and teenagers are huge fans, using fake tan runs the risk of creating stains all around the house. Bed sheets, underwear, the bathroom floor, collars, towels, swimwear and upholstery are all vulnerable.

Many stains will wash off, though I have had difficult staining on an upholstered bedroom chair, pale collars and a more permanent stain on my floor grouting which all needed more attention. There are stain-removal sprays on the market which are expensive and chemical-heavy, and why bother when we can sort the problem naturally with household items?

You will need

1 tbsp bicarbonate of soda
1 tbsp eco-friendly washing-up liquid

old toothbrush (for grouting stains)
clean cloth

In a small bowl mix the two ingredients together to a paste then massage into the stain using the fingers. Leave for 15 minutes or so then pop the item into the washing machine if practicable or wipe clean using a dampened cloth. For very tough stains and to ensure success, after treating the garment pop it into an old plastic bag, seal to keep it damp and leave overnight, then wash the next day.

For a grout stain I used the paste and an old toothbrush to scrub it until clean then wiped it with a clean cloth.

Oil Stains on drives and patios

A drizzle of oil from a piece of garden machinery on my pathway was really noticeable and grabbed my eye every time I walked past. It hadn't been there long and I don't know how it came to be there. There are products on the market that, apart from being expensive, contain harsh, harmful chemicals that will eventually find themselves in our eco system, so I decided to have a go myself.

It was winter time – I remember because I was out applying bicarb paste in the dark. I made a good dollop – 3–4 tablespoons of bicarb and the same of eco-friendly washing-up liquid. Then I applied to the oil stain and took an old long-handled kitchen brush and vigorously scrubbed it in – over and over.

I decided then to leave it – partly because it was nearly bedtime and partly because I saw no point in washing it off when it had just started to rain. I left it to the elements. The next day the paste had washed away, the oil stain was gone and I had a super-clean area of pathway.

Emergency Dog Clean

Out walking one glorious summer day in the countryside with my two dogs. This is my idea of bliss, by the way – I love it. However, Wilfred (a puppy at the time) encountered a pool of thick, black, oily tar substance (shame on the person who dumped it) and fell sideways into it. I have never seen such a mess and being in the middle of nowhere with no towel or cloth to clean him down with, I had no alternative but to walk home with a disgusting-smelling oily dog.

Once home I tied him to the gate post while I ran inside for a bucket of warm water, a sponge and a quick mix of bicarb paste. The bicarb paste was purely instinctive – I knew it would remove oil, knew it was harmless to pets, as long as I kept it out of his eyes and ears, and felt pretty certain it would destroy the disgusting smell.

On with the rubber gloves and huge handfuls of paste rubbed into the black oily patches on his legs and back. It was a panic situation and Wilfred behaved himself, standing perfectly still while I massaged the paste well in.

Grey sludge emerged as the oil released itself from his coat. A rinse with clean warm water and Wilfred was as good as new. I hope you never need bicarb paste for a similar situation!

CLEANING AIDS

The Luffa Gourd

Luffa Gourds grow on a vine belonging to the cucumber family and the fruit (also spelt loofah) is dried and then used as a natural luffa for the shower or bath and, in my case, used in place of the plastic scourer in household cleaning.

I would have loved to have been able to include the Luffa Gourd in my 'Time to Grow' section. I have made one attempt to cultivate it, but without success. I germinated four seeds from a packet of eight and then went on to nurture two huge plants. Unfortunately, neither produced flowers or fruits, but I will try again – though I think I need a heated greenhouse. Frustrated by my failed attempts (I shouldn't beat myself up too much, as it is a tropical plant that needs a long growing season), I decided to buy a pack of two.

I have to say I had my doubts. This pack of two compressed, dried fibrous fleshy lumps of the mature gourd (resembling shredded wheat in both appearance and size) didn't strike me as being robust and long-lasting. Just like shredded wheat breakfast cereal, once moistened with hot water (rather than milk) this natural genius is transformed into a pliable, tough, non-scratch scourer.

I was an instant convert. How could I ever doubt that Mother Nature had produced her own natural, biodegradable, effective, tough and long-lasting scourer?

The two luffas I have I use for cleaning. One for the kitchen – scouring pans, cleaning around the sink, etc. My second is used for the bathroom – great for shower screens! I remember thinking I would be content if my luffas gave the same life as their plastic sponge alternatives. You know how the green bit on the plastic sponge scourer becomes fluffy and ragged after a few uses and then joins the rest of the millions of sponge scourers in landfill? Well, if I tell you my luffas are still going strong after eight months . . .

I have had followers tell me, particularly from those areas that grow them naturally, the dried luffa will last a year – in fact, until the next season's growth. I have bleached mine using sodium percarbonate (green bleach) to clean and sterilize it, and it has been popped into the dishwasher too. Costing a couple of pounds, this is an easy, affordable switch to make.

Gloves

While on the subject of simple tools that aid cleaning, of course we all use cloths and brushes, and in addition I use gloves. Rubber gloves, though I am ashamed to say I don't wear them as often as I should, but on the plus side natural cleaning, I have found, is much kinder on the hands. I use others too, namely white cotton and exfoliating gloves. They are fantastic for certain jobs.

EXFOLIATING GLOVES These make cleaning so much easier when gentle non-scratch scouring is required. I wear a pair when cleaning brass and copper or badly stained items. It is easier to feel and get into every nook and cranny with a finger than the blunt corner of a scourer. A water- and limes-cale-marked shower screen can be polished up in a jiffy using the spray on page 235 and a pair of exfoliating gloves.

COTTON GLOVES These offer a quick, easy and non-messy solution when cleaning glass light fittings or chandeliers. I have two pairs. The first pair I wear then spray my gloved hands with all-purpose cleaner (if you don't already have the recipe, I give it again below), so that each hand is quite damp. I use the dampened cotton hands to then wipe every glass section, getting into each little groove. My chandelier was very dusty and I swapped the gloves around, right to left and left to right halfway through, giving me a clean part to work with. Once clean, change to the second pair of dry gloves and use these to polish the light fitting or chandelier to a sparkle.

Trying to spray cleaning solution directly onto a light fitting is not effective and probably rather dangerous, as water and electricity don't mix and most of the cleaning liquid drips off onto the floor anyway. Other than taking the whole thing down to dismantle, wash, dry and reassemble, this is my way from now on.

  60ml (2fl oz) white vinegar
  150ml (5fl oz) water
  40ml (1fl oz) surgical spirit
  20 drops of essential oil (lemon, eucalyptus, or perfume of
      choice)

For an all-purpose cleaner I simply mix all of these directly into a spray bottle.

DOUBLE BUBBLES

When it comes to the washing up, so many of us reach for the washing-up liquid bottle (dish soap), do a quick squirt then bubbles form and off we go.

One of my early switches to eco-friendly was washing-up liquid, having discovered that the back label of even the biggest brands contained the warning 'Harmful to aquatic life with long-lasting effects'. Living in a hard-water area I found I was having to 'double dose' on the eco-friendly alternative in order to get decent suds, until I made a discovery.

I had given my sink a sprinkle of bicarbonate of soda to remove tea stains, rubbed them off quickly and effectively with a cloth then rinsed it out in my bowl of warm washing-up water. Instantly, more bubbles formed, lathering up at an alarming rate. Of course, bicarbonate of soda is a natural water softener and soft water = more bubbles.

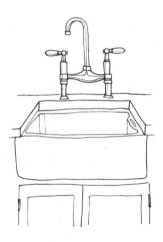

I now keep a sugar shaker of bicarbonate of soda alongside my washing-up liquid at the side of the sink. A squirt of liquid into the bowl then a sprinkle of bicarb, on with the tap and bubbles galore! I use half of the liquid I used to, the suds are long-lasting, the water, being softer, is kinder on my hands and I am saving money!

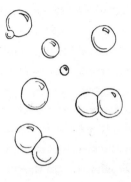

ODOUR OBLITERATORS

I am sure a pair exists in every household! That one pair of smelly walking boots, trainers, ski boots, football boots that, try as you may and as comfy as they are, stink!

Some youngsters wear their trainers and shoes without socks, which can result in damp stinky shoes at the end of the day. I have an old pair of comfy walking boots and I am not sure whether it is because they got very wet or whether the boots themselves are getting a bit old but they pong a bit. I have a friend who hired a pair of ski boots and loved them so much that after the week's skiing asked whether he could buy them. Trouble is, when he got them home the smell from them nearly blew the roof off!

There are products on the market that promise to keep boots and shoes fresh, though the root of the problem in my opinion is often due to the inside of the shoe or boot becoming damp with sweat or water and then being left to turn smelly and fusty because it didn't fully dry out.

Sweaty feet are normal – avoiding smelly shoes can be achieved by sticking to a couple of rules. Wear socks made from natural fibres (socks used to always be made from fine wool or cotton) rather than polyester or other man-made materials. Synthetic materials don't breathe and soon get smelly from perspiration.

Leaving wet shoes or boots in a cold damp place when not being worn will lead to them becoming smelly when you next come to use them. How many times are the muddy football boots left in the boot of the car or inside a kit bag only to find when they are next needed their smell is horrendous.

When shoes, boots and trainers are not being worn, try to remember to loosen the laces, pull the tongues forward and leave in a warm place that is well-ventilated so that they can aerate and any residual moisture of sweat can evaporate.

Here is my recipe for our own odour obliterators, costing pennies, which can be used over and over and will keep your boots, shoes and trainers fresh and gorgeous.

You will need

an old pair of tights or long socks
a few sheets of newspaper
100g (3½oz) bicarbonate of soda
scissors
essential oil for perfume (I use eucalyptus)

Loosen the laces of the smelly boots, shoes or trainers and set aside. Cut the two legs from an old pair of tights. Cut newspaper into 20cm (8 inch) squares – about 12 for each boot or shoe depending on the size (12 for an adult size). Scrunch up the paper pieces one at a time then open them out flat.

Into the centre of each piece of paper place 2 teaspoons of bicarbonate of soda and one or two drops of essential oil. Bring the four corners of the paper together and give a gentle twist to form into a small parcel. (Scrunching the paper first prevents it tearing or ripping as you make a parcel.) Pop the parcel into the toes of the pair of tights. Repeat, packing each parcel firmly into the tights until after around 12 parcels you have a length the size of the shoes or boots you will treat.

Tie off the leg of the tights to keep all of the paper parcels in place, then I form a loop using the rest of the tights so that

I can hang the odour killers up in the fresh air when not in use.

Place your new 'natural' odour obliterator in the inside of a dry but smelly boot or shoe when not in use. The bicarbonate of soda will neutralize the odour, the essential oil will perfume them slightly and trainers and boots will no longer be offensive weapons.

CLEANING CLOTHS

I used to be a huge fan of coloured microfibre cleaning cloths – I still have a few. I went on to read that they use many chemicals in their manufacture, and when they are used they release plastic particles into the water supply, so they are negative when it comes to being biodegradable but they do a good job.

I think I am a little late to the party as far as bamboo is concerned. I know many readers will already know how fantastic this material seems to be. Bamboo is a highly sustainable plant and can grow to full size in just three to four months, and because it is pest-resistant, it can be cut and will grow again, making it much more sustainable than cotton. Like everything, the more you know, the more there is to know, and certainly during the process of turning bamboo into fabric, like cotton, chemicals are used – some of which can harm the environment.

I believe there are plans being put in place to make the fast-growing bamboo process more transparent, regulated and more sustainable. I bought bamboo cleaning cloths, which I like, they wash well, do the job but I have to say, after reading around the subject, I am inclined to favour upcycling my old towels and tea towels instead.

My old yellow towelling dressing gown, faded, pulled and threadbare in places, which I cut up into squares and edge stitched, yielded 14 cloths and I know will now keep me in cleaning cloths for many years. One rainy afternoon, I bound several of these towelling cloths in blue binding, several in pink and the rest simply edged. I now have blue for the loo, pink for the sink and the rest I use as the best dishcloths, even though instead of white they are pale yellow, which took a bit of getting used to, though I boast that they tone in with the colours of my kitchen tiles!

I find myself trying to be 'greener than green' but then come back to the same conclusion – it makes more sense to simply make things last longer. I used to routinely replace dishcloths and cleaning cloths weekly – tossing the old ones into the bin or passing them into the garage for car cleaning. I now wash and reuse, as I know many readers will have done for years.

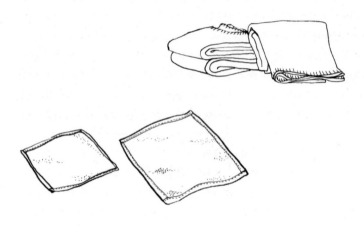

METAL CLEANING

Whether cleaning brass, copper or silver, the inevitable tarnish returns due to moisture and humidity in the air.

The return of the tarnish can be slowed down quite simply. Once the brass, copper or silver item has been cleaned and thoroughly dried and polished, smear over coconut oil.

Coconut oil is solid when at room temperature and I smear it over as though I was greasing a tin before baking. Using only my fingertips, I rub it into every nook and cranny. Then take a soft clean cloth and buff up the metal to return the shine, even though there will still be the slightest oily film, which will protect the metal from discolouring again too quickly. I used to clean my brass fender three or four times a year – I now do it once in the spring.

CLEANING FOOD

I am fortunate to have the space to be able to grow a lot of my own food, namely fresh fruit and vegetables, which require only a rinse in cold water in order to remove any surface dirt or grit and the odd wiggly creature. I know there have been no pesticides, wax or preserving sprays used at all.

The fresh fruit and vegetables that I do buy I wash thoroughly. Anyone that grows their own fruit and vegetables will know it can get frustrating. Greenfly, caterpillars, birds, fungus and rot can all take their toll, and the keen gardener has to be ready, vigilant and on their guard to deter predators by netting off cabbages, peas and cherries, keeping the growing area weed-free, fed and well-watered.

Compare home growing to the fields of crops seen nowadays. Not a weed in sight, not a rogue blade of grass. I see not one single leaf nibbled as each plant is a perfect-looking specimen with not a bird or caterpillar having left a tell-tale lacey hole.

Pesticides, insecticides, harmful chemical-selective herbicides and chemical fertilizers are used extensively and it is essential to clean our fresh foods before they are eaten – we are, after all, the end of the food chain. I was surprised to read that potatoes are treated with more pesticides than most any other crop, yet how many times have I used potatoes straight from the bag without washing or peeling.

I read a lot about how to rid our fruit and vegetables of any residual chemicals before we eat them and was surprised to see 'wash thoroughly' on packs of seemingly gorgeous supermarket apples. I read that rinsing in water will go a long way to removing any pesticide residues, adding one-part vinegar to three-parts water will kill bacteria and remove certain chemicals, but according to a study by the University of Massachusetts, good old bicarbonate of soda quickly and easily cleans your fruit and vegetables of up to 96 per cent of pesticides, wax coatings, bacteria and dirt.

You will need

bowl or sink
500ml (18fl oz) cold water
1 tsp bicarbonate of soda
colander

For every 500ml (18fl oz) of cold water, use 1 teaspoon of bicarbonate of soda, then wash the fruit or veggies by swirling them around freely in the water. Soft fruits such as strawberries and raspberries I leave for just a minute then transfer to a colander and leave to drain over a bowl.

Larger items such as apples, potatoes, pears, tomatoes and peppers I leave in the water for 15 minutes then remove, give a quick rinse in a bowl of plain water, and drain.

Wax coatings on apples and lemons can be removed by wiping them with a sponge in the water too. Very thick wax coatings on lemons will can be removed more easily using hot water rather than cold with the bicarbonate of soda. I prefer to buy unwaxed lemons if I can find them.

Probably the most efficient way to wash produce is when it is bought rather than as it is required. Only one lot of water and one lot of bicarb will be needed and it only has to be done the once, rather than having to add 'wash veg' as another task before every use.

A lot has been written about washing produce before eating. Some say water is enough, others advise adding vinegar or salt to the water, and other recommendations, like the study cited above, suggest adding bicarbonate of soda.

They are all agreed on one thing, though, and that is to wash before eating, even if it's just in plain water.

TIME TO GROW

This is not a gardening book. I know only a few Latin names for plants, but what I do know is how to grow fruit, vegetables and flowers. Growing food has been part of my life for what seems like forever, and my fondest memories as a child were spending sunny days (the days always seem sunny when you're young) with my grandad in the garden. He used to give me jobs – one of which was pricking the side shoots from tomato plants, and even to this day, when I do the same thing to my plants, that sweet green grassy smell from the leaves takes me back in time.

I am thrilled that so many people are interested and inspired to have a go at growing food themselves, and even if there isn't sufficient space in your life and home for rows and rows of veggies, it is surprising how much can be grown in pots. Even if you have a few herbs on your windowsill, you will save money with a handy pot of home-grown basil, rosemary or parsley to pick at rather than buying the supermarket plastic-packaged alternatives. A sunny balcony can keep you going in courgettes, tomatoes, salads and a few beans, and some strawberries can be grown there too.

This is a promise: if you grow food yourself it will not go to waste. Your time, toil, patience, nurturing, watering and care have helped to raise a carrot or parsnip with two legs, a split tomato, an oversized courgette or curly cucumber. You will be proud, they are precious and, as we know, while such foods can be rejected by supermarkets – yours instead will take pride of place and become an 'over dinner' talking point when served up on plates.

GROWING FOOD IN POTS AND CONTAINERS

Many readers may be wanting to get started but have neither a large garden nor vegetable plot. I am fortunate to have growing space but I decided to grow a selection of vegetables and fruit in small pots in a limited yet sunny space on my patio.

Here is a simple, and not too prescriptive, timetable if you fancy having a go yourself using your space, however small.

Plan in January and February. Look at the space you have then think about what you would like to grow. Salad leaves, radishes, spring onions, rosemary, thyme, mint, basil, tomatoes, French beans, runner beans, strawberries, courgettes and chives grew amazingly in pots for me. Choose your crops and buy the seeds.

Start in March and select a number of growing containers – pots large and small, wooden boxes, even metal cans and plastic bottles can all be suitable. Even though it may be too early to sow, the pots can be prepared for planting. Fill each pot with peat-free compost, ensuring there are drainage holes in the base of each container. If you use wooden boxes that may have huge slits, lining them with old pieces of cardboard will help them to contain the compost.

Arrange and place your pots in the sunniest spot. In late March and early April – really depending on the weather – most seeds will start to germinate at 15°C – begin to sow your seeds. Having decided on which crops to try, follow the instructions on the reverse of the seed packets. Alternatively, buy mini plants when you see them available in garden centres and supermarkets – usually from April onwards.

From now on you will be entertained almost daily as you see those tiny seeds germinate into the tiniest tender two-leaf seedlings, to then go on to yield amazing crops. A small container garden, as well as getting you outside to tend, weed and water will feed you and actually make you happy.

My container garden turned out the most beautiful display by the end of July, yielding salad crops, tomatoes, French beans, runner beans, courgettes, onions, garlic and a whole selection of herbs that could be harvested regularly and continued to grow up until the first frosts. Even the smallest space can look beautiful and every inch can be utilized.

Two courgette plants gave me a constant supply. If you are looking for a recipe that is just a bit different, utterly delicious and that will be happily eaten by those that say they don't like courgettes, is dairy-free and easily adapted to gluten-free, then my Lemon and Yellow Courgette Cake or lime green alternative can be found on page 143.

If you've never grown anything before or if you want to get children involved, start with a sunny spot, a few pots and a watering can. Buy one or two cherry tomato plants, a courgette or two and a supermarket pot of basil, thyme, mint or parsley can even be transferred to a more substantial pot and nurtured through the summer months. (See my upcycled plastic bottle herb planter on page 80.)

Success breeds success and the following spring you will be looking to grow more. You will be buying more packets of seeds as your confidence as well as your garden grows and by the following year, who knows? You will be sending for seed catalogues and including a small propagator on your Christmas list.

You may become inspired to try new and imaginative crops, too – I am going to have a second try at amazing Luffa Gourds (see page 265). You might even add your name to an allotment holder's waiting list!

Growing food is good for you in so many ways. There is the learning as you read about a whole new subject, the exercise as ground is prepared, the maintenance to keep weeds clear and plants supported and nurtured, the fun when crops mature and you begin to enjoy the fruits of your labours and the nutrition when you are munching away on the food you know has not been treated with chemical sprays or pesticides.

GROWING FROM SEED

I like to browse seed catalogues as others may do fashion mags. This is a winter job for me, sitting by the fireside and contemplating the coming of spring. Whatever your size of garden, patio, balcony or even an inside space, there is something you can grow.

Some crops use up lots of space whereas others use only a little and will yield lots of edibles. A cabbage or cauliflower, for example, will need around 60cm (2 feet) square, and once harvested, that's it. A dwarf green bean or kale plant, on the other hand, needs half that space and will keep producing beans and leaves as long as you keep picking them and for many weeks.

When deciding on what to grow have a look at the reverse of the packet and see how much space the seedlings need. A beetroot needs only around 10cm (4 inches) but celeriac need 50cm (20 inches)!

Seeds are costly and at first glance it seems an expensive hobby, but have a look at the 'sow-by' dates. You can usually grow plants from a packet of seeds for several years provided they have been kept in a dry, dark place. A tin with a well-fitting lid is perfect for storing your seeds. Parsnips are an exception to this several-year rule. However much I try I have not had successful germination from old seed and have always bought fresh every year.

Alternatively, if you are a parsnip lover and want to grow them every year, try leaving a parsnip in the ground to regrow the following spring, produce a tall stalk, flowers and then seeds. These tiny papery little things can simply be stored in a paper bag in August/September to be then sown early next spring.

I keep runner bean seeds, too. Leave a few pods on the plant at the end of the season to grow fat, then they go yellow and at that point I take them from the plant and leave them to dry naturally in the shed. The pods will split of their own accord and the dark, mottled, large purple seeds can be stored in brown paper bags for the following spring.

Try experimenting with seeds, saving your own from garden plants and not just veggies. The dried pods from sweet peas can be stored and used next spring. I took a picture of my sweet peas in full flower to know exactly which colours belonged to which seeds once the plants had died down.

I successfully germinate sweet pea seeds in cardboard tubes (toilet rolls and kitchen paper rolls) and then plant the whole lot straight into the ground in spring – the cardboard decomposes and the plant can spread and grow when and as it pleases. Sweet peas grow a long tap root and the long tube is perfect for them. To prevent the compost falling out of the end of the tube, simply pack down the first inch or so using a piece of wood, then fill the rest of the tube, sow the seed, water in, stand them side by side in a box and germinate inside in a cool light place in January or February.

Once the sweet pea seedlings are about 15cm (6 inches) tall with several sets of leaves, I pinch out the growing tip. This encourages bushy growth, more stems and more flowers.

The little pots of bushy green leaves can then be transplanted outside – these are hardy plants so cold nights will not worry them at all. I plant them out usually during May. They are fast-growing and will need the support of canes or trellis to hang on to.

Once flowering, it is important to cut the flowers daily. The more the flowers are harvested, the longer the plant will produce gorgeous fragrant blooms. If the flowers are permitted to form seed pods the flower production will slow down and finally cease, though, as already explained, at the end of the flowering season in early September seeds can be saved for next year – and so the cycle continues.

A healthy seedling needs light and it needs water. Many followers have sent me screenshots of their seedlings, delighted at their progress, assuming that big is best! The perfect seedling, however, needs to be fairly compact and perfectly formed. A long, pale, lime-green stem with small pale leaves at the tip is described as 'leggy', and this poor soul has been overdosed with kindness. It is probably too warm and is growing faster than it is capable of, searching for extra light and nutrients, hence the long stem and pale colour.

Most seedlings prefer a cool very light area (out of direct sunlight). A germination temperature is often given on the seed

packet – usually around 15°C. Watering is important but not too much, and a spray of water is often better for very young seedlings rather than complete inundation by the heavy duty rose of a watering can.

Compost

Seeds also need a growing medium – good earth or a peat-free compost. They need a container (if not being sown straight into the ground).

Composting is very exciting and can be a huge solution to many of our climate problems. Home composting and keeping waste out of landfill is something many of us can do. There are small kits that can be bought for those with very limited space, but even a box-type construction made from wooden pallets will make the perfect vessel.

The everyday waste items that go into my bin are fruit and veg peels, coffee grounds, tea leaves (I gave up on tea bags when I discovered the majority contain plastic), grass clippings, hedge trimmings, the contents of my vacuum cleaner, my biodegradable gift wrap (see page 209) and my Biodegradable Christmas Wreath (see page 123).

Obviously at the end of the season, the contents of the greenhouse – tomato plants, cucumber plants, etc. – join the compost, too. Plants with very thick stems and stalks I chop into 20cm (8 inch) lengths with the end of a spade to speed up decomposition. Autumn leaves also go into the compost bin.

I cover the compost bin with an old piece of carpet to keep in the heat, I water it from time to time and use a garden fork to give it a stir about twice a year. I remember one time giving my compost heap a stir, it was a cold day and I was wearing rubber gloves. The heat being generated from my bin was welcome on my cold hands. I ran in to get a thermometer to find the reading to be 28°C – the ambient temperature outside was around 6°C! My compost bin was happy and working.

You will know when your compost is ready – the loam (soil) is dark, crumbly and when you pick up a handful the smell is pleasing, just a warm earthy smell. No wonder plants love it. This rich, gorgeous growing medium can be used to fill pots, your greenhouse, to top-dress roses and shrubs, add to your veggie plot – in fact, I can never have enough of it. Peat-free compost can be bought in bags and until your own compost is ready to use (about a year) you will need to buy it to get started.

CONTAINER IDEAS

Have you browsed the garden centres and looked at the price of pots – especially non-plastic ones?! Spend a packet if you have the means, but I prefer to think outside of the 'growing' box at quirky alternative containers that are either free to us or at least a fraction of the price of fancy glazed alternatives.

I have grown seeds very successfully in single-use plastic trays that had a supply of blueberries, cherry tomatoes or grapes. Some, in fact, have a lid and drainage holes – a ready-made mini propagator for tomato and cucumber seeds.

When I was a child seed trays were always made of wood, and again one of my jobs with my grandad was to wash them with soapy water every spring and leave them outside on a bright sunny spring day to dry.

Seed trays for sale are now mostly plastic and while I have quite a number to reuse every year, I will not buy any new or replacements. I now search for wooden boxes of any kind for seed sowing.

SOWING AND GROWING SEEDS

Sowing seeds is quite straightforward. The seed packet will give exact instructions on how to sow and their germination time. Usually you scatter them thinly over a tray of compost, cover lightly with a little more compost and water in.

Once seeds have germinated in trays they need to be given more space. As they grow larger they will begin to crowd the tray and they will be using up any nutrients in their bed.

Pricking out is the term given to singling out each baby and carefully moving it to a bigger house with more food and more room to move about. A seedling is ready to move once it has its first set of adult leaves. This is when the first two leaves (and most seedlings look the same) show but then from the centre another pair of leaves will appear, which will look quite different to the first two – these are the adult leaves.

Fill the bigger pots that you are transplanting into with compost, ready for the seedlings. I then use a pencil point to gently ease under the root of the seedling. Always handle a seedling by a leaf. If you damage or bruise a leaf the seedling will survive, if, however, you pick it up by the tender stem and damage it the seedling will most certainly die. Pick up your seedling along with its roots and as much compost as possible. I always make sure my seed tray is well watered before pricking out, then more compost adheres to the root ball.

Make a hole with the pencil in the pot of compost and carefully lower your seedling into its new bed. Gently firm it down then water in.

When it comes to plant pots, plastic and terracotta of all sizes are my 'go to' for pricking out. I usually prick seedlings out into 7.5cm (3 inch) pots, but again, if you don't have these then single-use plastic yoghurt and cream pots are the same shape and size. Make at least one drainage hole in the base with a knife or scissors.

If re-using plant pots – plastic or terracotta – it is important that they are clean. A bowl of warm soapy water with vinegar added (one part vinegar to four parts water) will clean them of algae, dried-on debris, mould and stains, and in fact anything that could lead to disease.

This is a job that makes me realize that spring is on its way, as I take a bucket and old brush then wash my pots and trays and leave them to dry outside, usually in the weak February sunshine.

I have seen free used pots available at garden centres – plastic and the odd chipped terracotta – so keep your eyes peeled for a bargain.

TIPS: Head over to the Time for Craft and Creation chapter. You can make the most delightful decorated pots and give as gifts. Great to do with kids. See page 107.
Turn to the Time to Clean chapter – I have a cleaning process that will transform your badly stained yet precious terracotta pot to its former glory. See page 233.

GROWING FROM CUTTINGS

Many plants can be grown from cuttings, and following these few simple rules I would urge you to try anything that takes your fancy. A rooted cutting in a hand-painted pot (see page 107) will make the perfect gift, has cost nothing and I promise will be cherished by the recipient far more than a potted plant from a garden centre.

As an example, let's take my rosemary bush. It is long-established, looking a little woody to say the least, but before either cutting it right back or at worst digging it out and replacing it I decided to take a dozen or so cuttings. The cuttings rooted – 100 per cent success rate and I have gifted them to friends and family.

I have used this method to successfully root sage, lavender, lilac and various cactus houseplants. I would urge you to try any plant that has a fairly woody or firm stem.

You will need

rosemary or other plants

scissors

7.5cm (3 inch) plastic pots (a clear yoghurt pot is perfect to keep an eye on progress)

peat-free compost

cup of water

hormone rooting powder

a clear plastic tumbler or pot to place over the pot (to create a mini propagator)

Start by cutting sprigs of rosemary. Cut a 20cm (8 inch) length of new growth The palest-coloured leaves are the newest, and spring is the best time to do this.

Gently pull downwards on the leaves and remove the bottom three sets of leaves. The lumpy section where the leaves were joined to the stem are called nodes and this is the area where roots will grow from. Take the scissors and cut just below the second set of nodes, discarding the end of the stem. Pop this cutting into the cup of water and repeat with the rest of the cuttings.

Fill the pots with compost and firm down lightly. Take one of the cuttings and dip the tip of the stem into the hormone rooting powder. Some say rooting powder isn't necessary but I find it gives a better success rate (we don't need failure!). Tap off excess powder on the side of the tub then gently push the cutting to the edge of the pot. By sliding the cutting to the outer edge and using a clear pot you can then check on progress. Repeat with two more cuttings so that you have three per pot.

Water then pop a clear plastic tumbler or pot over or recycle a plastic bag secured with a rubber band.

My rosemary cuttings took exactly one month to grow roots. Lavender and sage can be rooted from cuttings in exactly the same way. Try anything that takes your fancy, remembering that in nature plants actually want to grow!

Once rooted well, the cutting can be moved to its own pot – start with a 7.5cm (3 inch) diameter pot then as it grows move onto a larger one or transfer it to a permanent spot in the ground.

REPOTTING

Whether it be a houseplant, well-established young plant, cuttings or patio plants, there will come a time, if it is thriving and healthy, that it will outgrow its pot. You will see roots appearing out of the drainage hole at the base, the leaves may be yellowing as it is starved of nutrients and at worst it may look as though it is dying.

I repot outdoors because I usually make it a messy business. Water the plant well before starting. A badly pot-bound plant can seem impossible to remove from the pot at first and may need some gentle toing and froing before it gives up the old house. Set the unhinged plant aside as you prepare the new residence.

Choose a new pot that is wider and taller than the original. Place a few stones or broken plant pot pieces (crocks) in the base to aid future drainage. Large outdoor pots can be stood on chocks (small pieces of wood or specialist wedges available to buy), which will lift the pot off the ground ensuring the plant doesn't get waterlogged, especially during the winter when the plant is dormant but the weather is not.

An over-watered plant can suffer just as much as one that is under watered, so excess water needs to be able to drain away freely. When repotting house plants remember to include a drip tray below the plant pot so that excess water doesn't run out and ruin a carpet or table (I speak from experience).

Top off the crocks in the pot with a few inches of compost then use the original pot set inside the new pot and fill the compost around it, firming it down as you go. Fill almost to the top then remove the original pot from the centre. You will have created the perfect hole to drop the plant's root ball into.

Transfer the plant, then firm down the soil around it and fill with extra compost to top-dress. Water well – the plant has been re-potted with very little stress and handling of the plant.

SPLITTING PLANTS

There are a number of plants that can be successfully 'split' to increase numbers. These are the plants that grow every year (perennials). Splitting should be done when the plants are dormant, for example in late autumn or early spring or when flowering has finished. The plants I regularly split are forget-me-nots, primroses and primulas, wild geraniums, lily of the valley, hostas, irises and agapanthus.

Small clusters of plants can be divided by simply lifting from the soil, cutting the plant in half with a trowel then replanting the two pieces separately and replenishing the soil. Some perennials can get huge and start to take over. In such cases I take out the whole plant and with a spade I ruthlessly chop the cluster into probably four pieces, planting the separate plants in a new place in the garden. Always water well after disturbing, but then you will see your plants flower with more vigour and health than they did as a large group.

Chives

I need to give a special mention to chives after seeing the smallest handful in the supermarket, packaged smartly in a single-use cellophane pack, weighing just 25g (1oz), imported from Europe and retailing at around 80p.

Chives are a wonderful low-maintenance perennial herb, can be split just about any time, though I tend to do it when their spiky leaves are just showing through in March. They will grow happily in a pot just outside the kitchen door and can be snipped almost daily and used in so many dishes. The flower buds can be used to make your own capers and the pale-lilac edible flowers make an excellent garnish. Anyone can grow chives, and they continue to give, will come back every spring, ask nothing of you and offer so much more than the mild onion-flavoured, green edible leaves.

Grow from seed or buy a small plant, or better still if you know someone with a clump of chives, they will split easily so that you can take a clump home. Chives will grow successfully in a pot and in any soil. The bright-green leaves will first appear in March and they will keep you going right through to the first frosts. In May, tiny dark-purple buds will appear, which are edible and make the best mock capers.

Chive Bud Capers

You will need
small jar with non-corrosive lid
60ml (2fl oz) white vinegar
½ tsp salt
½ tsp sugar
3 tbsp chive buds

Place the vinegar, salt and sugar in a small saucepan. Heat until the sugar and salt dissolve. Leave the liquid to cool.

Pop the chive buds into the small clean jar then pour over the cooled vinegar. Seal and store for one month before using.

Add to pasta or use in place of capers in any recipe and the One-pot Puttanesca on page 51.

Or leave the buds to open and reveal the most beautiful pale blue/purple flowers. The petals can be pulled out in little tufts and they make a gorgeous salad garnish – perfect to top off my green salad and crustless quiche on page 54.

Chives love to be clipped, and regular harvesting ensures the leaves will remain tender and luscious – I use chives in scrambled eggs, sprinkled over quiche before baking, added to salads and omelettes, stirred into cottage cheese, baked in with cheese scones, added to stews and soups, to top off the perfect jacket spud (see page 202). The possibilities are endless.

If your chives have not been harvested regularly – if you have been on holiday, for example – the plant may look yellow, limp and wilted, but don't be thinking that is it for the year. Gather up all of the yellowed leaves, tough flower stems and any rotted parts and give the whole lot a thorough haircut to about an inch tall. Place all of the cuttings on the compost heap. In next to no time you will see new bright-green leaves appear from the undergrowth and in a week or so you will be busily harvesting again right until the first frosts.

Your plentiful supply of chives in the summer can also keep you going through the winter, as they can be easily frozen. Simply clip washed and dried chives into tiny pieces with scissors, lay on a sheet of baking parchment on a tray then pop into the freezer for about half an hour or until they feel firm and free flowing. Transfer to a small freezer box and use as needed.

Alternatively, they can be dried. Use two sheets of kitchen paper and lay one on a microwave-proof board. Wash and dry the chives then clip into tiny pieces with kitchen scissors over a sheet of the kitchen paper, cover with a second piece of paper and microwave on High for just 20 seconds. The herbs will be steaming a little so lift off the paper, fluff them around, cover with the paper again then pop them back into the microwave for 10 minutes at just 100 watts – your machine's lowest setting – check and microwave for another 10 minutes. Check to make sure they feel dry, then cool and transfer to a glass herb jar for use in the winter.

Any plentiful supply of fresh herbs can be preserved this way – saving you a fortune during the expensive winter months. Most savoury recipes in this book include herbs as an ingredient, fresh or dried, so having a handy home-grown supply will save time and money.

Parsley dries and freezes very well using the same methods – I freeze the stalks, too, to use in stocks. Mint also freezes and dries well. Rosemary, sage, bay and thyme are hardy and will keep going through the winter. Basil is not a fan of the freezer. The delicate, tender leaves I have found lose colour and flavour, though their fabulous taste can be preserved in pesto, which can be frozen in ice cube trays (see page 30).

SPRING-FLOWERING BULBS

The first show of colourful spring-flowering bulbs is so delightful and heartwarming. We have the promise of longer warmer days, more colour to follow and it energizes us into sparking into action, clearing away winter debris and thinking about the spring clean.

Bulbs are the easiest plants to grow and can be great planted into pots to then give as gifts or to brighten up an outside or inside space, and they will continue to give you pleasure for years to come if you look after them.

I plant into containers usually in November. Fill a container (any pot, as long as it has drainage holes) half-full with garden compost or a peat-free compost from the garden centre. Pop in your bulbs (which look like onions) – the packet will tell you exactly how deep – then cover with more compost and that is it. Water lightly, leave outside and forget about them. During January you will see the first green spikes showing through and in spring they will provide you with the finest display of colour. Daffodils, tulips, snowdrops, crocus, narcissus – all are wonderful.

When the flowers have faded I remove the dead heads and move the pots of green leaves to an out of the way place to just be allowed to dry out naturally. The pots still need a little water so when the weather is dry during the summer, give them a sprinkle as you would everything else in pots.

By August the foliage has all but disappeared, so I remove what is left then either top up the compost, wipe down the pot, which may have got grubby over the months, or instead take out the bulbs and dry them in the sunshine. If the bulbs have little offsets, or baby bulbs, attached to the main bulb you can carefully remove these. The benefit of splitting bulbs is two-fold. The first is that you are immediately doubling your supply of bulbs and, secondly, if not split, after two or three years they can fail to flower or not flower as well. Bulbs like to be separated.

Once dried the bulbs can be stored in paper bags or, even better, onion nets, hung in the shed, the garage or other dry place then replanted again in November – and so the cycle continues.

Planting spring-flowering bulbs in the autumn in small decorated pots will make the most delightful Christmas gift that will not cost our earth! See tips on decorating pots on page 107.

Clusters of snowdrops in the ground can be split in early March once the flowers have faded but the leaves are still green. Dig up a small clump, separate the tiny bulbs, then move one or two together to a new spot. Pop them about an inch or two deep then you will probably forget all about them until next Christmas, when you see their tiny pointed leaves just showing through. What was once a delightful clump at the foot of our pear tree is now an impressive white carpet every January.

One of my favourite spring flowers is the aconite, and once established these will spread readily themselves. The yellow flowers go on to form seed heads and when I see these beginning to dry I tend to give them a gentle kick as I walk past to spread the seeds further. What was once a single plant given to me by my neighbour is now a huge yellow carpet of February gorgeousness.

BASIL

I love to grow basil from seed each spring. Once two sets of the chubby little leaves have formed they can be pricked out into separate pots. As the weather warms up the plants will grow quickly and profusely. I nip out the growing tips of my basil plants to promote sturdy growth and bushy plants. Keep the tips for use in salads or to go towards home-made pesto (see page 30).

Just twelve pots of basil will keep me going all summer long and I will also be able to make pesto to freeze to use during the winter months.

STRAWBERRIES

The sublime British strawberry! Fresh summer strawberries used to only be in season for a very short six-week period when I was a child. Back in the day, before the single-use plastic container, they were sold in woven straw baskets – how wonderful, yet not appreciated at the time.

Britain is now self-sufficient in strawberries from May to October. Around 70 per cent of the strawberries grown in the UK are produced by British farmers and I have to say imported fruits do not compare at all when it comes to appearance or taste. Strawberries can easily be grown successfully by the amateur in pots, tubs, hanging baskets or in the ground. Strawberries are also very friendly when it comes to producing ready-made cuttings for you. A strawberry plant will throw out long runners that go on to produce a baby plant, which can then be planted without the need for rooting powder.

When choosing strawberry plants, look for a thick collection of lush green leaves promising lots of growth. Strawberries are hardy plants and will sit in the ground or in pots in the worst winter weather. The spring arrives and they will begin to thrive, producing lots of greenery followed by white flowers in May and ripening red berries in June and July.

Strawberries need little attention other than plenty of water when fruits are forming and protection from birds who manage to spot ripe berries before you do. I have a wooden-framed netted cage that sits over the strawberry bed. To keep the fruits clean, protect them from slugs, suppress weeds and keep the ground moist it is worth tucking straw around the base of the plant and under the forming fruits. I didn't bother one year and a thunderstorm splattered each berry in grit and earth. Wet fruits can easily rot too.

The best fruiting years for a strawberry plant are the first three to four. In order to maintain a continuous supply for the future it is necessary to plan ahead. Towards the end of July and through August, or when your strawberries have finished fruiting, you can do one of two things. If the plants are in their first two years and no new stock is needed, take a pair of scissors and give the plants a good haircut. This may seem brutal, but simply gather the plant's leaves in the left hand, hold them up and cut the whole lot to about 7.5cm (3 inches) high. You will be left with a stumpy, sad-looking plant but within a few weeks new leaves will have started to grow from the base and the plant will look healthy and compact before the autumn arrives.

If you are wanting new stock, the plant can be left to throw out runners. The strawberry plant will do this naturally and young healthy stock will do this before fruiting too, so keep a close eye and cut them off – all the strength is required for fruiting.

After fruiting the runners can be left to grow and at the end of a runner sometimes up to 30cm (12 inches) long a baby strawberry plant can be seen growing at the end. The plant will search for a place to root, so simply placing a pot of peat-free compost underneath the baby plant is all that is required to grow new strawberries. I have found that burying a pot into the ground and anchoring the runner with a hairpin or thin hooped wire keeps everything secure.

In just a week or two the baby strawberry will have grown roots and established itself in the pot and at this point it can be cut away from the mother plant, who can then have a haircut in preparation for autumn and winter. The cutting can be left in its pot outside until the following spring when at first signs of growth in March it can be transplanted to a bed, a bigger pot, hanging basket, given as a gift – the possibilities are endless.

A growing space however big or small can be a happy place. So even if you are limited to a sunny windowsill, a balcony, a small patio garden or a large landscaped area with raised beds, greenhouse, cold frames and the like, there will still be the wonderous produce, the birds nibbling, the bugs wriggling and there are the good years and the not-so-good years, as I remind myself that even after three sowings I couldn't get a crop of peas this year.

There is something for every age group, every ability and, for me, growing both food and flowers is a much more worthwhile, productive, non-boring physical workout than a paid membership to a gym.

TIME TO THINK

decided to include a reflective chapter because the pressures of everyday life don't always allow us to step back, sit down and have a think.

We all have good days and not-so-good days. The good days are amazing. Things go well, the meal that you planned was perfect, your garden is looking resplendent in the sunshine, the house smells clean and fresh, even your hair looks good. You are feeling inspired to try something new! You are walking on air! You might try making lavender bags, upcycling an old towelling dressing gown and wondering how many cleaning cloths you can create. You may make a batch of puff pastry – you feel like the perfect 'home maker', really on a roll, planet Earth will be so proud of you!

Then there are those other days – the cake was overbaked, it's okay but I know I can do so much better, the meal I made was pretty awful if I'm honest, potatoes lumpy and the carrots still hard. I walk into the garden after the storm to find my finest broccoli plant has blown over, lying defeated on the ground, the house is knee-deep in dust and I won't even mention my hair. The news on the TV spreads more doom and gloom about the plight of our planet, broadcasting lurid tales of ever more destruction, unbelievable weather events and warnings that the Earth is in danger.

What is the point? Why do I bother? This is exactly the time when I know I need to and take a break. Give in a little – and give yourself a bit of a cuddle. It may be a hot bath or shower, a walk with the dog, a delve into a book, a bike ride, a run, or watching a good film. Have a think and take a breather.

Remember the good days wouldn't be half as good if they happened every day, because we would just get used to them and expect a good day to get even better. We have to have the flat days to balance things out, so just accept and give into them and ride them out – that's what I do! 'Pick yourself up, brush yourself down and start all over again' – I say to myself, because there is no one else that can do this but me.

Having good friends, family, a partner and just people to talk to is essential, but then it is important to listen as well as talk. We all know someone who never asks about you – who just prefers to talk about themselves all the time.

I think to be able to look in the mirror and like what you see is essential. I don't mean hair, makeup, looking beautiful, youthful, fresh and gorgeous – I mean to *like* who you see. Are you fair, kind, generous – you know yourself what your feelings have been and whether they feel good or not. You know whether you have been the best you can be that day and sometimes negative feelings come about when you know you have not been your best with someone or something. I think you know what I mean.

The best therapy for me is the outdoors, being around animals and soaking up the seemingly smooth running of the natural world. Everything out there seems to rub along nicely, whether that be the plant world, insects, animals, birds. However, I do see them squabble, so it's not just humans, and when I see it happen I understand how unpleasantness can be tiring.

There is a blackbird that hangs around the base of our bird feeders to catch the seeds that are disturbed by the smaller blue tits, robins and sparrows that are able to feed from them directly. There is an abundance of seed, enough for all the ground-feeding birds, but this one blackbird spends his time chasing off any other bird that dares to come near and pinch 'his' seed. I realize he is missing out – there is enough for him and all the other birds but he chooses to spend his time being angry, guarding his patch when he could have great fun meeting new friends, sharing and just being kind. I am sure he must use more energy chasing, squawking and being angry with other birds rather than adopting a 'live and let live' approach. The small birds maybe think 'why doesn't he like me?', when the truth is, he doesn't seem to like anyone.

When I get negative or hurtful comments on social media or in daily life – and believe me, one negative comment can upset the whole day – I just think about my blackbird. The angry one is the one missing out! I am simply one of those birds being chased away that day.

Interestingly, when my hens are let out of their run they always head straight for the bird feeders to enjoy the spoils on the ground. The blackbird disappears, the little birds return and they all feed happily together. The bully blackbird stays out of the way when the jolly giants come around. Watching birds and their behaviour around seed feeders is a great pastime and if you fancy making one of your own head over to page 86.

ENTERTAINING

Does the idea of having friends or family over for food raise your stress levels? You know you need to do it, they have invited you so many times, but feeling you are unable to do a job as well as they do adds to the stress even more. When I was many decades younger I had friends that used to invite us over for food. Their house was unbelievable (in my eyes), so much food, the tableware all matching and beautifully arranged. She was the perfect hostess. Pre-dinner drinks were offered, great food served outdoors in the summer yet cosy and candle-lit in the winter. The drinks cabinet contained bottles I had never heard of let alone tasted.

The experiences of dining at their house did absolutely nothing to raise my confidence. I hadn't the money to supply an array of drinks, I didn't have matching tableware and who had ever even used a tureen? My cooking and baking skills were adequate but how could I ever compete with this? That is where in my younger years I was wrong – this was not a competition!

Our two houses were different and, looking back, this was very much a show house – very perfect and very lovely. I was always shown the very latest purchase or acquisition and smiled longingly and enviously at the many wares. I did finally pluck up the courage to invite them over. They arrived and following a deluge of apologies and excuses over there being limited choice of drinks, the meal being a very ordinary casserole and sorry but it's only a crumble for pudding – we settled down to what turned out to be a very memorable and happy evening. There was lots of chatter, laughs and relaxation. The feedback was 'how did you not get stressed, and you were with us the whole evening and not in the kitchen, how is that even possible?'

After that night I learned a lesson about 'trying to keep up with the Joneses'. I don't bother!

Inviting people into my home is about sharing how I live, not aspiring to be something I am not or trying to be something I might think they expect me to be. There will always be those that are able to surround themselves in materialistic fineries, the latest in fashion trends, badged from head to toe in designer labels and know the best brands for just about every product. They can splash the cash and while I am not knocking it, I know some people like to live this way, have the means and find genuine enjoyment in it, but for me I know it could never work. I find richness in other ways.

The 'rich' people for me are those that have a breadth of knowledge, feel absolutely fine when they show up more than once in the same outfit. They can chat interestingly about things that they know, yet they are good listeners too. We have all sat in the company of someone who spends the whole time talking endlessly about their beautiful children or, even worse, about themselves. Rich people, in my opinion, are polite and pleasant, their homes are clean and wholesome, and not necessarily showing off their magazine-quality soft furnishings and this year's colour palette.

It took me years but I urge you to learn to be comfortable in your own skin and surroundings. Envy brings only a feeling of discontented or resentful longing for someone else's possessions, qualities or luck. I am fortunate that in the past I was taught by my grandmother to become resourceful and prudent. I can sew, knit, cook, bake, grow food, craft a few bits and enjoy trying to live a sustainable life.

I hope that now armed with the tools in this book the reader can start to live that way too.

We all need money, of course we do – it is no fun being hard up. I didn't have a lot of it so it never got the chance to become a huge motivator, whereas saving it did. If I could save £1 here or 50p there, I did it and the truth of the matter is, those habits never die. They stay with you forever.

What I am trying to say is please don't waste your life and valuable time on comparisons. Be inspired and motivated but don't be envious or jealous. Things don't always seem fair but in time everything evens itself out – you'll see. Your time and your health is limited, so make it work for you the best you can.

TIME TO BE ME

This is when I take time out to just be me. I am not wife, mother, granny, friend, cook, gardener – I am thinking about me. I look back over the years and realize I wasted so much time thinking and worrying about issues or people I could not change – and I still do, but to a much lesser extent.

Dog walking is what I love to do – it is simple, outside, exercising, head-emptying freeness. I find I can walk for quite some time and not actually remember much about it. I'm sure my head is simply emptying itself and while it is downloading doesn't update with any new data.

I have also discovered over the years that if I feel drab my output is drab. Whereas if I feel I am looking the best I can, output improves. This doesn't mean I am 'dolled up' to clean the bathroom and toilet – quite the reverse. I will clean in my scruffiest of clothing, no makeup, hair not done – but afterwards when everything is done and sparkling I will clean myself up, tidy the hair, on with clean clothes, a touch of lippy and I am ready to take on the world, even though I am probably staying in the house. Have you ever noticed that on the good days the jobs just keep on getting done? I cherish those days.

Lockdown was a real test – how easy would it have been to not bother getting dressed? I'm not going anywhere and I know I wouldn't be seeing anyone, but for me it was even more important to keep on top of things if I was to keep on top of my thoughts and feelings. I know Nancy too well and allowing her to 'go drab' would have had led to her feeling low and slow.

Life has become fast and challenging but it is also very short, so don't waste it worrying about things you can do nothing about. I worry for the future of our planet and really do believe that the change will come, some maybe from what governments, heads of state, conferences, rules, regulations and targets achieve, but effective and longer-lasting changes can be made by me and you.

I understand where I have gone wrong over the past fifty years, but so few of us knew the impact we were having on our precious planet, its resources, wildlife, weather systems, etc. There is no time to waste, so whatever your life is right now – one change, any change, will make a difference.

Going back to the opening chapters – where did I find the time to write this book? My motivation was born from the daily reminders from the media about the dangerous plight faced by our planet.

I honestly believe many of us want to make changes but in ways that are honest, don't rely on having to be persuaded to buy expensive 'eco'-friendly products – these changes have to be easy and to begin with they must be small.

This book documents the changes I have made in my everyday life, which over the past few years have stacked up to now be something more meaningful. Some of the day-to-day changes have been easy because it was about going back to the ways I used to do things before my reliance on single-use items. Other changes have been more challenging, involving trials and lots of errors before I got them right.

I made the time to write this book because fundamentally I really believe it is the right thing to do. I have found ways to do things differently. The cooking and baking recipes I have chosen compromise on time and money but not on taste, the growing section I hope helps the reader to understand the benefits of home growing even in a limited space. I have turned certain items into usable objects rather than dumping them into landfill. A number of craft ideas using everyday items continue to interest me and sharing them I hope may interest you too.

This book is a continuation of my journey to a sustainable but achievable green lifestyle, where I try to think about doing things differently, being less reliant on consuming and taking from our planet. My motive always is to look at ways to repair, replenish and heal our precious home.

I truly hope this book saves you some time as you begin to do things differently. I want you to create space so that you can do other things. Please take pride as you realize you waste less and then give yourself a huge thumbs up when you understand that you are also smartly saving money and the planet.

For me, the satisfaction I get on a daily basis is from knowing I am doing my very best to be honest, reliable and responsible to the generations that will follow.

I am learning to be the master of my time, energy and our planet's resources . . . I will not waste it!

CAKE TIN CALCULATOR

See page 130 for a full explanation on how to use this handy table. For example, if you're following a recipe for a 20cm (8 inch) round tin but you are using an 18cm (7 inch) round tin, multiply the ingredients by 0.8 to give a cake of the same depth.

Tins that you have in your drawer

	Round in inches		Square in inches	
Recipe Round Tin				
6 inch / 15 cm	**6**	**1.0**	6	1.3
	7	1.4	7	1.7
	8	1.8	8	2.3
	9	2.2	9	2.8
	10	2.7	10	3.5
	11	3.3	11	4.2
	12	3.8	12	5.1
Recipe Round Tin				
7 inch / 18 cm	6	0.7	6	0.9
	7	**1.0**	7	1.3
	8	1.3	8	1.7
	9	1.7	9	2..1
	10	2.0	10	2.6
	11	2.5	11	3.1
	12	2.9	12	3.8
Recipe Round Tin				
8 inch / 20ccm	6	0.6	6	0.7
	7	0.8	7	1.0
	8	**1.0**	8	1.3
	9	1.3	9	1.6
	10	1.5	10	2.0
	11	1.9	11	2.4
	12	2.2	12	2.9
Recipe Round Tin				
9 inch / 23cm	6	0.4	6	0.6
	7	0.6	7	0.8
	8	0.8	8	1.0
	9	**1.0**	9	1.3
	10	1.2	10	1.6
	11	1.5	11	1.9
	12	1.8	12	2.3

For example, if you're following a recipe for a 23cm (9 inch) square tin but you are using an 18cm (7 inch) square tin, multiply the ingredients by 0.6.

Tins that you have in your drawer

	Round in inches		Square in inches	
Recipe Square Tin				
6 inch / 15 cm	6	0.8	**6**	**1.0**
	7	1.1	7	1.4
	8	1.4	8	1.8
	9	1.8	9	2.3
	10	2.2	10	2.8
	11	2.6	11	3.4
	12	3.1	12	4.0
Recipe Square Tin				
7 inch / 18 cm	6	0.6	6	0.7
	7	0.8	**7**	**1.0**
	8	1.0	8	1.3
	9	1.3	9	1.7
	10	1.6	10	2.0
	11	1.9	11	2.5
	12	2.3	12	2.9
Recipe Square Tin				
8 inch / 20ccm	6	0.4	6	0.6
	7	0.6	7	0.8
	8	0.8	**8**	**1.0**
	9	1.0	9	1.3
	10	1.2	10	1.6
	11	1.5	11	1.9
	12	1.8	12	2.3
Recipe Square Tin				
9 inch / 23cm	6	0.4	6	0.4
	7	0.5	7	0.6
	8	0.6	8	0.8
	9	0.8	**9**	**1.0**
	10	1.0	10	1.2
	11	1.2	11	1.5
	12	1.4	12	1.8

Acknowledgements

My green journey started with a few simple switches and here I am now writing the acknowledgements for my third book – I am overwhelmed.

Following the success of *Clean & Green*, *Green Living* is the next leg of my journey.

After 'going green' on cleaning, it became apparent to me that by working that bit smarter with a raised awareness of the way I was living my life, I could, without a lot of effort, save money, save time, waste less, use less and in turn be looking after our planet.

I have so many people I need to thank and will be ever appreciative of their input.

Firstly, to my publisher Pan Macmillan who signed me up for this second book. In particular, the fabulous team at One Boat and most of all – Hockley. This book has been steered and kept on track with an ever so light touch and gentle nudge here and there. Hockley is a star, always professional, always encouraging and with a superb eye for detail, a quality which I always value and admire.

My agents and friends at Yellow Poppy Media who for the last seven years have helped, managed and facilitated my work commitments. Their continued belief in me and my vision has been so valuable. They have always been available at any time day or night to advise and support me – I thank you girls.

I am delighted and humbled by the comments from those early reviewers who agreed to put time aside to read the book. Who would have ever have thought that a northern lass, who has been around a good long while, would, in her sixties, be able to call herself a *Sunday Times* top ten bestselling author?

My followers – I doubt there would have been the motivation to write this book had it not been for their continued support and their genuine 'green' commitment. Equally, I would like to thank those who offer up their own ideas and problems. Together with those followers, through research and discussion, I have broadened my horizons and gained more knowledge which is now encapsulated within the many pages of this book. They have sent me fantastic comments and success stories as they themselves have stepped into a green way of life.

To my family and friends who now recognise that 'going green' is not my latest fad or something that I will get fed up of. In fact, between you and me – I am delighted to note that they are quietly and slowly converting to a greener life themselves.

Finally, to Tim (him indoors), who reminds me every day about what is important in life. He helps and encourages, deals with the paperwork and does everything else that has had to take a back seat when I am busy working. When I get out of bed at 6am and tiptoe downstairs to start writing, he inevitably pops in quietly half an hour later with a pot of hot tea. It is those little things, isn't it?

Thank you all so very much. Please enjoy the read – I have loved writing this book.

I hope you try the recipes, embrace some of the different ways of working and find the tips and hacks really useful. It's a good feeling knowing that changing the ways we do things not only saves time and money but also helps our precious planet. I believe small changes now will benefit our children, their children and their children's children.

Nancy

Author biography

Nancy Birtwhistle is a Hull-born baker who won the fifth series of *The Great British Bake Off* in 2014. Nancy worked as a GP practice manager in the NHS for thirty-six years until she retired in 2007. Motivated by protecting the planet for her ten grand-children, Nancy decided to change how she used plastic, single use products and chemicals in her home. Sharing her tips online, she amassed an engaged international following of devoted fans interested not only in her delicious recipes, but also her innovative ideas and time-saving swaps that rethink everyday household chores to make as little an impact on the environment as possible. Her book *Clean & Green* was a bestseller.

Connect with Nancy on Instagram: @nancy.birtwhistle, on Twitter: @nancybbakes or through her website: nancybirtwhistle.co.uk

Index

Notes

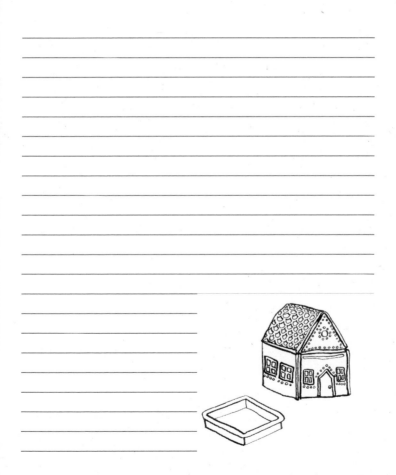

Also by Nancy Birtwhistle

'Nancy's enthusiasm and energy shine through. . . I have learned loads from this book!'

Aggie MacKenzie, co-presenter, C4's *How Clean is Your House?*

'From baking, to gardening, to organization, resourcefulness, and just her incredible energy ... she creates art out of everything in her life, and takes so much joy in the process.'

Jonathan Van Ness, *Queer Eye*

Looking to clean up your act when it comes to looking after your home?

Former *Bake Off* winner Nancy Birtwhistle is here to help. In *Clean & Green*, Nancy shares the simple recipes and methods she has developed since making a conscious effort to live more sustainably. Nancy's tips are cheaper, faster and easier than many of the go-to products and methods most of us currently use, as well as being much better for the environment and our waterways. Inside, you'll find more than 100 tried-and-tested tips and recipes, including zero-effort oven cleaner, kettle descaler, miracle metal renewal, toilet magic, pest control and flower food. From all-purpose cleaner, nature's freebies and fixes for problem-clean areas to effective replacements for harmful chemicals, as well as planners and to-do lists, Nancy's tips and ideas will keep both your home and the planet clean and green for future generations.

Available now.